Audio Made Easy
(Or How To Be A Sound Engineer Without Really Trying)

by Ira White

ISBN 0-7935-7293-2

HAL•LEONARD®
CORPORATION

7777 W. BLUEMOUND RD. P.O. BOX 13819 MILWAUKEE, WI 53213

Visit Hal Leonard Online at
www.halleonard.com

CONTENTS

CD TRACKS

Tracks	Title
1.	INTRODUCTION
2-9.	CHAPTER 3/INSTRUMENTAL EQ & MIXING
10-16.	CHAPTER 6/EQ FREQUENCIES
17-20.	CHAPTER 7/DIGITAL EFFECTS
21.	CHAPTER 8/COMPRESSION
22.	CHAPTER 9/SPEAKER PHASE
23.	CHAPTER 12/FEEDBACK CONTROL
24.	IN CLOSING
25.	LIVING FOR TOMORROW
26.	WHEN GOD IS FOR US
27.	AUTUMN PORTRAIT

1. INTRODUCTION

THIS IS YOUR BRAIN…THIS IS AUDIO…THIS IS YOUR BRAIN ON AUDIO

As far back as I can remember, people have been asking for a complete book on professional audio that they can understand. Unfortunately, most books only cover certain aspects of audio, and are wrought with pages of formulas and abstract elements that tax the interest of the average person in a world where most would believe transient response is what you get when you ask a bum a question. Or that Hertz is just another car rental company. Not exactly.

A lot of people want to get involved in sound or recording for the fun and fulfillment of it. They're not interested in writing a thesis for their doctorate. They're probably not going to be asked to design and run a system for Whitney Houston. However, they *would* like useful information, a sense of accomplishment, and some aural excitement without too much pain (Hertz?). Beyond that, audio interests can be pursued as far as the heart desires.

So I decided to write this book covering a little of everything without becoming too tedious. It's based on experience and the many questions asked of me by colleagues and customers, and it delves a little deeper into some of the more misunderstood areas such as using EQ, speaker specifics, and recording techniques. In it, I wish to furnish real world solutions and tips that will show results and not just raise more questions. I wish to accommodate a variety of equipment budgets and provide a firm foundation on which to build audio wisdom. I wish to give you the capability to soar to new heights, and achieve any lofty dream you may hold dear! I wish to retire at age fifty with lots of money!!

Well, maybe I won't get that far, but at least we can accomplish something along the way. I'm game if you are.

I r a   W h i t e

P.S. You'll notice some numerical indicators next to certain audio terms. These are listed in the index at the back of the book, and refer you to additional related sections on the topic being discussed.

Also, even if you're only interested in a particular aspect of audio, I encourage you to read this whole book. There are tips and information within every section and application that should be helpful to you. Besides, it isn't that long. In the time it takes to add a room addition to your house or take a French vacation, you could have read this book and still had time for a shower. (I'm assuming you're a slow reader.)

This is a work of non-fiction. The characters, incidents, and dialogues are products of the author's imagination but are not to be construed as unreal. Any resemblance to actual events or persons, living or dead, is entirely intentional though probably grossly exaggerated.

2. SOUND PSYCHE

THE PRIDE AND THE PASSION

Music is an art, and engineering is just an extension of that art. You should first understand that you are an integral part of the overall product — not just a button pusher, but an artist that makes spontaneous decisions based on what you hear. The song is the subject, the instruments are the paint, the tone and balance are the brush strokes, and the room (or recorder) is the canvas. Your equipment ultimately gives you the capability to create the overall picture, to skillfully mix the colors, to move yourself and others to an emotional response. And like any passionate endeavor, the fact that you are working hard and starving at the same time is mostly hidden by the enjoyment of your quest.

The only problem is that you need to master the basics well enough for them to run on automatic while you dedicate your time to creating. Like riding a bike, you can concentrate on where you're going and not on how to turn the pedals. And you need to feel comfortable and confident in your capabilities, especially in one-shot live situations. Just as in scuba diving, if you panic you drown. Don't be intimidated and keep a cool head. Things are rarely as bad as they seem, and you'll find that peace of mind promotes good judgement and will rub off on others around you creating a sense of security and trust. That's a positive influence on the most volatile variable of working with others — chemistry.

Like riding a bike, you can concentrate on where you're going and not on how to turn the pedals.

THE GOLDEN RULE

. . . and speaking of chemistry, I'd like to mention something about social interaction. When working with other people, the fun can quickly depart if we eccentric artists get into adversarial relationships. We often try to push our opinions on others which only puts them on the defensive. We all need to work together, but I still need to know that I'm in control of my responsibilities.

The way I do this is to always try to show concern towards another's views. Sometimes they're right. Sometimes just politely explaining when they're not, in overly-technical jargon that neither of us can understand, helps. In either case, I'll generally make a point of periodically (and sincerely) asking how things sound to those concerned. Once their defenses are down and they feel secure in having received sufficient consideration, I can maintain reasonable control in peace. Mutual respect develops. Everybody wins. In those exceptions where it doesn't work, blackmail is a nice backup plan.

THE BROKEN RULE

I'll be passing on ideas in this book that will establish constructive guidelines. The ironic thing is that once you've mastered them, it's time to throw many of them out. Rules can't teach you how to create, but only how someone else created. It's up to you to blaze new paths. Once you've got a little knowledge tucked away, you'll find that common sense goes a long way towards experimentation and discovery. And once you've beaten every new idea to death, you'll invariably learn that less is more.

I never fully realized how this had applied to my engineering development until I tried learning about stage lighting. I read about focal lengths, lumens, ellipsoidals & fresnels, Roscolux colors … I was so proud of my wealth of knowledge. And then I saw an Emmy-award winning lighting guy do almost everything with a few par cans and four basic colors. I should have asked him how he did it without the other junk, but he probably would have said, "Sounds like you've been reading a book."

So don't let rules hold you back. And don't over complicate things. Keep it simple, keep an open mind, and don't hesitate to ask questions. You can learn something from everybody, and each little tidbit can be filed away in your cerebral library of audio wisdom to be called upon in critical decisions when you least expect it. As soon as you stop testing the limits, you will go no further. Have fun, be young, drink Pepto Bismol.

3. THE SOURCE BE WITH YOU

If you want specs, get a spec sheet. If you want detailed features and operation, get an owner's manual. But if you want excellent general info and brilliant tips. . . me, too! Hopefully, we'll take the mysticism out of audio equipment and learn how to use this stuff, taking each in its proper order of signal flow. We begin where it all starts — at the source.

ON THE LEVEL

There is a great variety of sound producing instruments which you will most likely be dealing with in your audio aspirations, many of which are already electronic in nature. These include tape decks, CD players, stereo or instrument preamplifiers, keyboards and sound modules, etc. These can plug straight into appropriate audio equipment and transfer their sounds directly and accurately. Acoustical sounds such as vocals and acoustic instruments cannot. They must first be changed into electrical energy to be used, so we add an incredible variety of microphones to our list of sources to accomplish this task. Using which-ones-where will be discussed shortly.

Our first concern is levels. Though all these products lack the higher voltage to move speakers (amplifiers do that), they nevertheless have a low level voltage that we can express in a unit of measure called the **decibel** (or **dB**) that will let us know how potentially loud each can be in relation to the other. Their dB output rating, or *gain*[1], will be important when integrating with other equipment and can be classed in two general categories — **mic level** and **line level**.

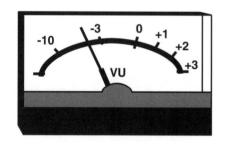

Mic level sources are the lowest, and generally associated with passive sources (those not driven by AC power). Microphones themselves are typically in the -60dB to -50dB range, electric guitars around -30 to -20dB. Line level sources (keyboards, stereo equipment, mixers, etc.) are above -20dB, are usually AC powered, and can get up to +4dB average peak (or *nominal*[2]) output. Now check the meter on a cassette deck while listening to a tape. You'll see that the meter may read from about -20dB to +4dB (a 24dB range), and there is a big difference between the loudest and softest stuff. Now imagine adding another -40dB to the bottom range for a total of 64dB between our lowest and highest sources, and you can get some idea of the great variations in equipment levels. But be not dismayed for, miracle of miracles, the mixer we use will allow us to accommodate for these differences.

MICROPHONES

Mic choices can be one of the hardest decisions because most people don't get the chance to compare many out in the real world. There are usually three or more nice choices in the same class, though one will most likely have the nicest sound and/or price to set it apart from the rest. Knowing which one takes a little bit of research. As with most products, the more you spend, the more likely you'll get higher quality. But these days, there are some top-notch mics in almost every price range, so don't let budget kill your expectations.

When shopping for mics, compare through good speakers (preferably studio monitors) or try to get them on a trial or return basis to make sure they live up to your real world needs. Listen for a smooth and musical sound. One mistake is to gravitate toward mics that have the most treble and bass in their response. This can indicate undesirable peaks or a lack of mids. The ideal should be to have a natural, balanced sound as the starting point. Then you will have all the necessary sonic components to manipulate as your heart and ears demand. Also check handling noise by tapping the casings, and off-axis rejection by talking into the side of the element which can determine how well it rejects feedback. All in all, you'll discover some pretty significant differences from mic to mic. Now, let's cover some information on microphone types.

A **dynamic** mic is a little speaker in reverse. Soundwaves in the air vibrate the mic diaphragm, moving a tiny coil back and forth around a magnet and generating a low voltage signal. Dynamics are durable, economical, and have good response within close distances. Though they have limited sensitivity for picking up distant sources, this can be a plus in live sound where isolation is critical. This means the mic doesn't pick up things you don't want it to. Good affordable dynamics are around $100 to $300. Some standards include the Shure SM58 and Beyer M69.

A **condenser** mic is designed with a more sensitive diaphragm for increased frequency response and distance pickup. Unlike a dynamic mic, it generates signal through a change in capacitance between two charged elements, and requires a voltage source to drive circuits in the mic or an associated electronics pack. (Don't worry, I'm not sure *I* understood what I just said.) The voltage needs to be supplied by an integral battery or an external source called **phantom power**[3] which is available on most professional mixers. (No, it's not a power boost for your system!)

Condensers are necessary in critical studio applications, but used less frequently in live sound due to higher cost and somewhat more fragile components. I also personally find the handhelds a bit sensitive for live vocals, lacking the isolation and feedback rejection of current quality dynamics like the Audix OM6. Economical cardioid condensers like the Audio-Technica AT33R or AT4033 can range from $200 to $500 respectively, while various switchable pattern and tube circuit models run from $500 to $2500. Less expensive battery-operated condensers can be had for under $150 and will do okay in budget situations, but lack the quality and level handling of the phantom-powered models. There are also special miniature condensers designed for choirs, podiums, conference tables, and other live applications.

A lesser known design is the **ribbon** mic, made by just a few manufacturers. It gets its name from the very small, thin metal ribbon that serves as its element. Though sensitive like a condenser, it is passive (non-powered) like a dynamic and has a very low output level. Besides being expensive, its delicate ribbon is easily prone to damage. You won't see these very often and they aren't essential in any particular application, though they do have a unique 'warm and sweet' sound.

EXPLORING THE POLES

Mics are available in a variety of pickup, or polar, patterns. **Omnidirectional** mics pickup sound in all directions making them unsuitable in most live applications where directed pickup and **feedback**[4] rejection are crucial. Consequently, **unidirectional** mics (which includes ball mics) are designed with special vents allowing sounds from the rear and sides to enter the capsule and be cancelled. Be aware that if you wrap your hand around the head of a unidirectional and cover up its vents, you turn it into an omnidirectional that's prone to feedback! Another uni trait is called **proximity effect**. If a source such as vocal is within 6" of a unidirectional mic, bass frequencies become unproportionately higher in level. Some mics have a bass rolloff switch to compensate for this, or it can be controlled at the mixer EQ if the sound is boomy or muddy.

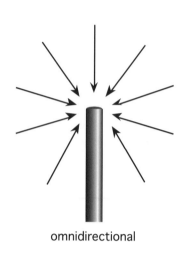

omnidirectional

unidirectional

Cardioid design unidirectionals have a medium pickup pattern around the front and the greatest rejection of sound at the rear of the mic. **Hypercardioids** are usually more expensive and have a tighter pattern making them less prone to feedback, with greatest rejection to either side of the rear. (One of the most affordable is the Audix OM3.) **Supercardioid** is tighter still and designed more for narrow distance pickup, many times in the form of long 'shotgun' condenser mics. **Bidirectional** is a rarely used pattern that picks up from both front and rear with greatest rejection on either side. It is only available in special design dynamics and in studio condensers with switchable patterns.

MIC TECHNIQUES

Since most of you will probably not be in an ideal room environment, I choose to focus on close micing techniques. With a good studio condenser, any instrument will sound natural when picked up from 3 feet or more, but you'll also pick up bad room acoustics, noises, and any other nearby instruments with the extra level required. Close-micing sounds more 'in-your-face' and is definitely necessary when isolation is important, but mic placement is critical. This is because it takes a little bit of distance for tones from different parts of an instrument to finally mix to become its complete sound. The bigger the instrument, the greater the distance. The trick in close-micing is to pick up a part of the instrument that best represents the whole thing. Subtle or subjective corrections may be accomplished through mic choice or mixer EQ.

If you choose to **stereo mic**[5] distant sources for recording, you can use a simple "V" configuration. Place the heads or bases of the mics together (not touching) to form an angle of 75°-90°, each one aiming toward opposite sides of your source area. I like the bases together because the separated elements offer a little more stereo imaging while mildly simulating the distance between our ears with a lot of air in between, a typical characteristic of sound engineers.

Now we get to the part where common sense goes a long way. *Where should the mic be placed?* Where the instrument sounds the best. *Where does the instrument sound the best?* Listen to it, Sherlock.

Acoustic Guitar: Let's start with a guy playing acoustic guitar. First, listen to the guitar from about 3–5 feet away. This natural sound will be your reference. (If it sounds like junk, forget this step and say your prayers.) We'll be placing the mic 6" to 12" away from the front so the picking hand won't hit it. Now pretend your ear is the mic, and listen around all the spots within 12" in front of the guitar. If it sounds too dull, don't put the mic there. If it sounds too thin or hollow, ditto. If it sounds about right, put the mic there, Goldilocks. . . you're ready to roll. My favorite spot is to the side of the soundhole at the end of the fretboard in front of the high end strings. For close stereo micing, I'll prefer another somewhere around the bridge of the guitar.

First rule: *trust your ears.* (You didn't know you had all the answers stuck on the side of your head, did you?) Choose a spot with the sound closest to what you're looking for. The only drawback is if you have no clue as to what you want to hear. Solution: start listening to a lot of good music and develop preferences. *Your* sound is probably written in your DNA and you just need to draw it out.

For acoustic guitar, a good condenser is preferred for stage or studio. Built-in pickups can be more convenient for live use, but they don't reflect the natural sound for critical recording. However, it can be nice to record both mic and pickup combinations to take advantage of both — the natural sound of micing and the unique tone and isolation of the pickup. If you're feeding the pickup direct through long lines such as a snake (an 'extension' cable of multiple mic lines), use a **direct box**[6]. I've also used a good wireless lavalier in live situations with some excellent results. Clip it on the soundhole in such a way that it's not setting in the hole and EQ as needed.

Electric Guitar: With electric guitar cabinets, you have the same situation as with an acoustic instrument. Tones come from the center and sides of the speaker cone, the port, and the cabinet itself. Listen close to areas of the speaker and you'll notice that the sound isn't the same 5 feet away. A particular problem I've found is that many guitarists have their cabinets on the floor with the higher frequencies shooting under them in a narrow pattern. They adjust their tone for the very 'warm' sound they're hearing while high end 'bite' is actually cranking out at speaker level. This is why many guitar rigs sound so thin and edgy from the mic and audience perspective. Better that the speaker is raised or angled up so the guitarist can hear and adjust his tone more accurately.

It's up to you to decide whether you want the distant or close sound or a combination of both, and mic accordingly. I usually mic within 6" at the side of the cone pointing toward the center, and control the 'edgy' treble by cutting back on the mixer high EQ. This brings out more of the guitar warmth. Another ambient mic can be placed back 5 feet or more for studio recording if desired. My favorite mics going up the price scale: Shure SM57, Audix OM3, Beyer M69, Sennheiser 421, or a *large diaphragm* studio condenser.

Though I prefer to mic, electric guitar can also be run direct to the mixer especially when used with a guitar preamp designed for this purpose. The problem with direct guitar is that optimum tone can often be dependent on the combination of everything being processed and punched through a guitar rig, particularly when it comes to distortion. Experiment. Direct or otherwise, you may find the unique sound that makes for an international star . . . or draws complaints from the neighbors next door.

Bass Guitar: I almost always favor running electric bass direct. There are rarely distortion effects to deal with, and you get accurate and isolated pickup of the instrument. Once in a great while in the studio, there comes along a bass rig that sounds so fantastic that it would be a sin not to let the rest of the world share in the experience. In those cases, I will most likely use one of my better electric guitar mics and combine it with the direct signal for added flexibility. If it's a good bass, this should be one of the easier instruments to capture well.

Drums: This is the toughest single undertaking for most engineers and requires the most resources. And because drums collectively cover the broadest frequency range of any instrument, it shares a place with vocals as one of the most critical parts of your mix. I suggest a minimum of six mics and a compatible mixer with at least 3 bands of EQ^7, one sweepable, on each channel. (If you're already intimidated, it may be time to run out and buy a drum machine. You won't be the first to give in.) If it's a less critical situation or you're a purist, you're off the hook. Set up a stereo pair of good condensers in front of the set and you'll get that natural sound. Add an optional mic on the bass drum if you wish to control and accentuate kick.

Individual drums require close micing to isolate them from each other and give us more control of the mix. Placement is best just over the edge of the top head within an inch or two. When desired tone can't be achieved with the proper mic, placement, or drum tuning, it can be assisted by the mixer EQ. I'll offer some notes based on my drum micing experience and EQ techniques which are discussed further in the Mixer chapter if you get confused. After becoming more familiar with using EQ, you may then wish to refer back to these notes. Or you may regard them as useless suggestions for what you're attempting to achieve. Your choice.

Many engineers use *noise gates*[8] on mics to isolate drums, and sometimes they may be necessary. I prefer not to use them for several reasons. Most isolation problems can be controlled by mic choice, placement, or EQ. Also, some bleed from other mics can give the drums more of a live sound when balanced effectively. So don't feel it necessary to run and buy out the noise gate stock at your local music store. Better to use the money for better mics.

Bass Drum: This requires a specialized mic like an Audix D4 or AKG D112 to handle the excessive air pressure and low frequencies. It should be placed inside the shell within 6" of and aimed towards the beater head to maximize critical high frequency attack. Low end without the high frequency attack is just a dull chest-pumping thud. (You can demonstrate by jumping off the sofa onto your butt.) Some potential problem areas: excessive bass below 100Hz, muddiness in the 100–300Hz range, and/or a need for more attack around 2–4kHz.

Snare: Any of the mics listed for electric guitar (except the large studio condenser) are appropriate for snare. The major problem here is bleed from the high hat, especially if the drummer is crazy enough to use Rude cymbals! I minimize this by using a hypercardioid and pointing it away from the hat at the edge of the snare under the first tom. Placing the head of the mic at the edge allows it to pick up more of the snares and high mid 'crack' from the shell. Placing it in over the snare head will usually result in more of a dull pop, forcing you to boost high end and increase hat bleed. Problems may be a dull or hollow bump in the 300–600Hz range or a need for more high end from 2–6kHz. In the studio, it's a nice idea to mic the bottom head as well to control snare balance if you have the resources and extra tracks.

Hi Hat: Mic this with a condenser pointing straight down a few inches above the outside edge opposite the drummer. Isolation is generally not a problem, but I prefer to roll out all frequencies below 1kHz to eliminate noises, and boost above 12kHz for a sweet high end.

Toms: Mic just over the outside edge pointing across the head with the same type mics used for snare. You may need to roll out some dullness in the 200–400Hz range. Add high end at 2–5kHz. If I'm experiencing some bleed from large cymbals, I'll use the higher frequency to keep them from sounding harsh. If you have to pick up two toms with one mic, pick the smallest toms and use a cardioid mic with good low end. For a fat sound on floor tom, I'll sometimes use a bass drum mic to accentuate the lower frequencies.

Overheads: Use a good condenser in the middle of the set about a foot above the highest cymbal. If two mics are available, use a stereo pair angled out toward opposite groups of cymbals. I always roll out everything below 200Hz to keep the low end tight. Frequencies up to 1kHz may also be reduced to maximize cymbal pickup and minimize ambient pickup of the set. In smaller live venues, you can often eliminate overheads since the cymbals will carry and may get picked up by vocal mics anyway.

Percussion: Use overhead-style micing for this. Dynamic mics will do okay for things like congas and cowbells. Live setups can also be picked up with a good lapel (lavalier) mic, wired or wireless, on the percussionist himself allowing freedom of movement with the various instruments. From the chest location, point the lavalier downward instead of upward if it's a unidirectional.

Acoustic Piano: Trust your ears and listen around the instrument for the sweet spots. The safe and accurate bet in solo grand piano recording is a stereo pair of condenser mics placed 3–5 feet away with the piano lid full open. Of course, with the distance involved, room acoustics are going to be more critical to the sound. So in less than ideal environments or when isolation is crucial, you need to mic inside about a foot high and angled towards each side of the soundboard to equally pick up low and high strings. If the mics are too low, strings closest to the element will peak on you. If you want a brighter sound with more attack, move the mics forward toward the hammers. (For isolation in a group performance, try to position loud instruments like drums farther away from the piano.)

In live sound, I've found it possible to get a reasonably balanced sound and good isolation from a single unidirectional condenser if the grand is a 7 to 9 footer. With the lid at the lowest open position for isolation, place the mic on a boom over the strings about halfway in from the side. The mic should be pointing to the back, parallel to the soundboard with the rear of the mic over the hammers. Height should be close to the lid without touching it. The reason this works is that the mic is directed to the back to maximize bass and warmth, while the normally peaky mids and highs are off-axis and rejected for a smoothing and balancing effect. It's not as effective with a smaller grand which lacks the additional warmth and bass to balance with the higher strings. Some EQ may still be necessary to compensate for low mid resonance off the soundboard and lid. This is usually cut somewhere between 250Hz and 400Hz. Some dynamics or flat condenser *boundary* mics like the Crown PCC-160 do okay, but I avoid using omnidirectional PZM mics.

When it comes to uprights, I've never found it feasible to mic from the top. In the studio, I favor removing the front board and stereo micing each side like a grand. In live situations, it's more convenient to mic from the rear. I usually find that the second opening in the frame from the bass side gives me a decent sound with a single mic pointing right into the rear soundboard.

Orchestra: To capture that natural quality I keep talking about, orchestral or band instruments should be mic'ed from at least 1' and ensembles or sections at least 3' away. The distance also minimizes the 'edginess' of strings and the mechanical noises of some instruments. In performances, isolation doesn't take priority over proper mic placement, and some ambience or bleed can actually add dimension. The greater concern is to keep the louder instruments such as percussion or brass away from the softer and lesser-projecting instruments like piano and strings.

In recording, you could just stereo mic the room to capture a performance as the audience hears it and eliminate mixing altogether. In fact, a stereo pair in a good concert hall should be my primary tracks even when multitracking. In that case, these mic techniques would allow for subtle and individual control of sections where needed. For solo instruments in bands or ensembles, there are a number of small clip-on mic designs available for wired and wireless applications.

Strings: Like acoustic guitar, stringed instruments are relatively low in level and require the most consideration in pickup and isolation, so always try to use a good condenser. For a single violin, viola, cello or string bass, point the mic towards the bridge and F-hole area. For ensembles, center the mic over the group and slightly angle it away from louder instrument sections if necessary. Treat harp like an acoustic guitar and mic individually from the side at a point equidistant from the strings and soundboard.

Reeds & Woodwinds: For isolating 1 or 2 instruments, you can mic near the end or bell. With ensembles, center above the group as with violins. Flutes will always be picked up from above. Good dynamic mics will do okay for small groups of 2 or 3.

Brass: Dynamics will work here, too, if it's all you have available. Since horns are directional, be sure to get enough distance on sections for a good blend of the whole group. French horn can be mic'ed from above and behind. (So why do they stick their fist in the bell? I think they're stashing something in there.)

Percussion: Due to the extreme frequency ranges involved from timpani to bells and cymbals, always try to use condensers. I can usually cover the whole section with 1 or 2 distant mics, so I tend to concentrate placement on making sure I get a full sound on timpani since the high end stuff usually cuts through.

Vocals: Most of the microphones made are designed with vocals in mind, so there's no shortage of choices. I prefer dynamic mics in live applications to avoid problems that can occur with 48 volts of phantom power going through a stressed handheld mic cable. Most of the time, you won't have to worry about mic technique or placement since the performer is going to eat the mic anyway. Just hook them up, pass out the teriyaki sauce, and set 'em loose. The rest, God willing, will be done at the mixer.

In the studio, you'll hopefully have more control. Definitely use a good condenser here and try to keep the performer at least 3" away by offering him a Big Mac ahead of time. Another method is to use a nylon pop screen set in front of the mic which will help control breath pops as well. If the mic has a low rolloff switch, use it to further reduce muddiness or pops.

Harmony: There are two ways to mic harmony parts. One, as you have probably already figured out, is to mic each singer giving you the most isolation and total control of the mix. In multitrack recording, this can be done one voice at a time to allow a singer to concentrate on his/her part alone. The other way is to use one mic for multiple singers (maximum 3 per mic). In live situations with a small vocal ensemble, this will allow them to control most of their blend naturally so they can't blame you for poor balance.

I prefer the stereo pair setup in the studio, because it gives me the natural dimensional imaging of everybody being in a unique position in the mix due to placement and room ambience. I can wrap up to 10 singers in a semi-circle around the mics. The biggest problem is when singers just aren't good enough to perform their parts well together. Then it's back to one track at a time.

Choir: This is more of a problem due to the sheer number of people and the distance of the mics from them. Always use unidirectional condensers. With the availability of more economical condensers and choir specific designs, it isn't necessary to buy the more expensive studio condensers for live use, and they can be a disadvantage with their high sensitivity more prone to feedback and picking up extraneous noises.

I space out one mic for every 4 or 5 people across, 2 or 3 rows deep. (More rows may require additional rear mics, or just stick all the bad singers in the back and don't worry about it.) Assuming you're about 6' tall, stand on the first row and stretch your arm up in front of you at a 45° angle. I want the mic head just beyond your fingertips with it pointing at the back row. This method gets the mic closer to the overall source, picks up the back rows on axis, and slightly rejects the closer front row which would otherwise tend to be much louder.

For more conservative sound situations such as recording or when you're not competing with orchestra or band levels, you may be able to cut the number of mics in half or use a stereo pair and place at a slightly greater distance for a natural blend.

Podium: Just a quick note regarding speaking mics. Just as with choir, there are small special design condensers for podiums. Many are not designed for very close pickup, and may be overloaded by powerful voices within 6". Unless you prefer the sound quality of a heavy metal band through a Radio Shack PA and the wind noise of a class 3 hurricane, consider substituting a quality handheld in those situations where some prefer to dine on the podium mic.

I spent a lot of time on this section because it's where it all starts. If you screw up here, you'll never fully recover later on. Mic technique is a common sense art, and will make everything else easier if done right. A final point would be to use mics like a light. Do you need a floodlight to cover a wide area? Do you need a narrower spot beam to project a little farther into the darkness? Where would you point it to illuminate things best? Mics work the same in reverse: *omnidirectional* = lightbulb, *cardioid* = floodlight, *hypercardioid* = medium spot, *supercardioid* = narrow spot. See the light?

4. UNPLUGGED

THE WONDERFUL WORLD OF WIRELESS

Hop on down to the local PA store, pick out an economical wireless mic, hook it up to your sound system, and let the fun begin! Unfortunately, as with most technological tools, this concept can fall right in there with E.T.: The Extra-Terrestrial and fast food that's good for you. Nobody promised audio geeks a rose garden, but my initial experiences even fell short of compost!

My introduction to wireless systems was in music retail back in the '80s. Unfortunately, we were dealing with primitive low-cost systems which, at that time, all performed horribly. I naturally assumed poor quality, annoying sounds, signals dropping out, and frequent breakdowns were unavoidable aspects of wireless. That's why I lost faith, at least until I eventually heard some good wireless systems in the $1500 range. Finally we were getting some performance though such cost was still prohibitive for many consumers who needed these convenient tools—especially churches and local theatre that required multiple systems. The good news is that prices on quality wireless systems have been coming down over the years.

Nonetheless, we still had an abundance of unexpected problems to arise as we combined multiple units, used them in different environments, and integrated them in various systems. It seemed our troubles had only just started. So began my long quest for truth based on research, trial and error, and numerous soul-stirring revelations usually preceded by incredible stupidity. This chapter is a by-product intended to help you get more out of wireless microphone use, especially those models in the under $1000 range, and bring you up to date on some features, price ranges, things to look for, and potential problems to avoid or overcome.

I also want you to be aware of features that I've found to be most practical and dependable in wireless design. Some companies have done a good job of addressing many needs in design and performance, and I would only encourage other manufacturers to show the same common sense and attention to detail in their product development. Let me go down my personal dream list:

1. Though the standard receiver chassis need not be rackmount, all should be *rackmountable* with optional "rack ears" or an available rack shelf. Rackmounting reduces abuse and possible damage to the unit and its connections, offers security and convenient transport for multiple systems, and looks nice too. The receivers should also be designed for easy and stable vertical stacking when not rackmounted. A metal chassis is preferred over plastic.

2. Antenna should be mounted on the *front* of the receiver, not on the top or rear, to accommodate rackmounting or stacking. It's hard to believe there are companies still making rackmount units with antenna on the rear where they can't be extended in a rack. They may inform you that an optional front-mounted **antenna distribution system** for multiple receivers is available for a few hundred dollars. Appropriate response: "I've only got one wireless, but it's comforting to know I can spend even more money for something I shouldn't need and can hook up other units that I don't have." Since antennas can suffer damage, they should be easy to replace without major surgery.

3. Receiver output should be variable *line* level for better signal-to-noise ratio, especially when patched through longer lines or snakes. Mic level outputs are simply not necessary with the input flexibility of most current mixers. Having both 1/4" phone and balanced XLR connections is always a plus, and a related ground lift switch would be a welcome feature to eliminate **ground loop**[11] hums. Since a lot of economical receivers use AC adapters (wall-warts) for their power, I would prefer the option of a compatible **power distribution** unit that will use one plug and supply power for four to eight systems. (Alternately, there are rackmount AC strips like the SF10PC by Kaman for under $150 which will accommodate up to six adapters.)

4. Since lavalier mics possess the greatest failure potential due to cable stress at both mic and connector points, they should be easy to repair, economical to replace, or both. I've found lavs for $25 that sounded as good as $100 models and held up better. One cost-effective design by Azden utilizes a right-angle mini-phone plug to maintain a low profile less prone to stress against the body and eliminate the sharp "u-turn" of the dangling mic cable. An appropriate relief feature for straight plugs would be connections on the underside of the transmitter instead of the top. Or simply providing a metal belt clip that can be flipped upside down would offer both options. (Are there any wireless manufacturers listening here?) And wouldn't it be loverly if all the wireless manufacturers adopted a standard right-angle plug, and made all mics and packs interchangeable? Hint, hint...

5. Transmitter LEDs should stay on for continuous "active" indication as opposed to the instantaneous blink of most systems. A multicolor LED might be designed to change color, say from green to yellow, when the battery grows weak. All transmitters should have *silent on/off*, not the annoying "thump" evident on many units. And an on/off cover on the transmitter (like that on Sennheiser's Evolution series) is nice for avoiding accidental shutoff in theatrical presentations.

A WIRELESS OVERVIEW

Take a microphone and hook it up to its own miniature radio station, and you'll have a wireless mic system. This is comprised of a battery-operated transmitter that the mic is connected to, and a receiver that passes the signal on to our mic inputs. Just as radio stations must transmit on different frequency channels, you need a different channel wireless system for each mic to operate them simultaneously.

VHF, or **V**ery **H**igh **F**requency, wireless systems use the 169MHz to 215MHz frequency range. Manufacturers generally offer about 15 to 20 VHF channels but for each two systems you use, other "spurious" frequencies are created by their combined signals. By the time you get to eight, the air is getting a bit cluttered with frequencies. Too many can cause interference from receivers getting confused as to who their partner is. Nevertheless, I have used up to 12 carefully-matched systems without much problem.

UHF, or **U**ltra **H**igh **F**requency, systems in ranges up through 900MHz offer much tighter reception allowing more to be used without interference problems between them. In fact, Broadway shows may use as many as 32 or more! (Shoot, the battery budget alone probably rivals what the government pays for a hammer.) Unlike VHF, most UHF have user-switchable frequencies so you can change to another channel if a problem arises with one. Good UHF systems start at about twice the cost of VHF, running from around $500 up. Be aware that cheaper models are typically limited to around 8 compatible channels that aren't switchable, so they're more prone to interference problems.

Non-diversity VHF systems use a single receiver antenna to pick up the signal, and will realistically transmit at least 50' indoors. (There are no non-diversity UHF that I know of.) <u>**Diversity**</u> wireless, usually $50 to $100 extra in VHF models, are dual-antenna/dual receiver systems that improve reception range up to 100' indoors. There are a few cheaper, non-diversity **dipole** VHF

systems out there with two antennas for slightly stronger reception, but these are tied to only one receiver.

The farther away the transmitters and receivers are from each other, the weaker the signal. Problems arise from sheer distance or when original and reflected transmission signals arrive at an antenna simultaneously canceling each other out and resulting in a loss of signal. With a diversity system, if one receiver loses the signal, the other will take over without any conspicuous break in the audio. In the event of poor reception, elevating a receiver or placing it closer to the transmitter is the best solution. Balcony locations are good since they offer more elevation and unobstructed line-of-sight to the transmitters.

Since other **RF** (radio frequency) sources can sometimes interfere with wireless operation, receivers have a **squelch** or **mute** control that can be adjusted to reject "stray" frequencies when signal is lost or the transmitter is cut off. (I'll discuss other simple ways to address this problem along with squelch adjustments in the Troubleshooting section.) Other typical receiver features include an RF indicator showing transmitter reception, audio indicator showing peaks or levels, and *gain* or *level* controls on both transmitter and receiver.

Wireless **lavaliers** are "tie-clip" style mics used primarily for speaking and theatre, though they can also be effective for some creative micing including acoustic guitar (clipped on the high-E-string side of the soundhole) and mobile percussion players (clipped on the percussionists themselves). Lavalier systems utilize a battery-operated beltpack module for the electronics and transmitter. Mics are available in omnidirectional and unidirectional models. Most people think that, as with handheld mics, a unidirectional pattern is best for lavaliers because it is less prone to *feedback*[4]. However, due to the chest or head (in theatre) placement of lavalier mics, there ends up being little difference in the feedback potential between omni and uni patterns but considerable difference in the way they perform.

Since unidirectionals are designed to reject distant and off-axis pickup to reduce feedback and increase isolation from background sounds, uni lavalier placement ends up rejecting the voice as well necessitating increased gain to restore vocal level. As a result, feedback potential is increased (especially in the higher frequencies) and the gain at the mic element itself can be up to three times louder than an omni. This makes the unidirectional mic much more subject to noises such as breath or wind, rubbing of clothing, or microphonic noise from the cable itself. (If you ever hear a pastor's broadcast with a lot of extraneous breath and clothing noise, you know the soundman made the mistake of using a unidirectional lavalier.) A final problem with these mics at the chest location is a greater tendency to lose the voice when the user turns his head, another shortcoming of rejection. The solution: use an omnidirectional.

Wireless **handhelds** have self-contained transmitters in their handles, and **headworn boom** mics use a beltpack module like lavaliers. Unidirectional patterns are typical here, especially for musical programs where more level and isolation is demanded. Despite an untraditional "Wendy's drive-thru" look, many pastors are also switching from lavaliers to headworn mics for extra level,

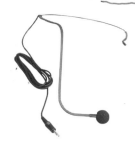

tighter sound, and less feedback. To avoid the more apparent problems with breath pops, proximity effect, and conspicuous appearance in these speaking situations, the few 'near-invisible' *omni* headworns available like the Countryman E6 are a recommended option. Be aware that no headworn should be placed directly in front of the mouth, but at the corner of the mouth or a little below.

Though Lectrosonics and Azden started the trend, most wireless companies now make a small transmitter module that will plug into the base of any normal mic and turn it into a wireless. This design doesn't compromise the sonic integrity of the mic casing itself and gives you more options on mic choices. I've even used modules on miniature podium condensers for cable-free wireless operation in the middle of a floor. It can also be an economical upgrade to wireless using mics you already have.

TROUBLESHOOTING

Reception: The first concern with wireless setup is making sure you get strong and consistent reception of the mics. As I mentioned before, most single antenna (non-diversity) systems are dependable indoors within a 50' range and dual antenna (diversity) within a 75' to 100' range, in spite of the fact that most specs tell you they're good for 200' to 1/4 mile. Of course, this is under perfect conditions: the Bonneville salt flats on a clear day with no sunspot activity. (Frankly, I can't even recall the last time Billy Graham had a crusade there.)

I prefer setting up receivers at my mixer location so I can see the RF indicators and know when the transmitters are active, but there have been some situations where I placed receivers near the stage and ran their signals through an audio snake due to problems with space limitations, distance, or potential interference from digital audio or multimedia equipment at the mix position. The main concern here is having the extra lines from the stage and making sure they're **balanced**[10] connections either available on the receiver or achieved with a ***direct box***[6].

Place the receivers for maximum reasonable elevation, and make sure antennas are fully extended. If you have some minor dropout problems, try experimenting with antenna angles such as one vertical, one angled. Also, with many lavalier and headworn transmitters, the mic cable doubles as an antenna, so make sure it is relatively straight and not bundled or coiled up while in use. I'll run you through a series of reception checks in the next section.

Interference: This stuff can be mysterious. Sometimes interference sounds like irratic distortion, noise, or static. Sometimes it sounds like mic feedback, though it's distinguished by multiple tones that fade in and out and are not constant like feedback. It can also result in momentary static when the transmitter is cut off, the effect of an instantaneous interference before the receiver has a chance to mute after losing its signal. You may only notice this with *silent on/off* systems since many brands have an inherent pop when the transmitters are cut off.

In any case, interference is a point where the receiver is trying to receive another renegade signal from somewhere else either when the transmitter's signal is lost or weak, or when the stray signal is just too strong on that particular frequency. Though it can be caused by other wireless, offenders include a few TV broadcast frequencies, power transformers, and digital equipment such as CD players, synthesizers, and effects units. I've had situations where two wireless systems of different brands and frequencies interfered with each other, where a digital lighting board caused problems with particular channels, and a system in a church at the other end of the block was picked up almost 500' away! Sometimes you just have to exchange the system for a workable frequency, but there are a few preventatives or quick fixes to pursue first.

When it comes to VHF, never buy a wireless system that transmits on local TV broadcast frequencies. (The stores should have a manufacturer's list of such frequencies.) It is really the responsibility of the wireless dealer and manufacturer to collaborate on ordering only those systems that avoid local stations, and to make sure any multiple systems you might have or add are on compatible channels. But you can avoid problems by raising the issue and making sure they don't sell you the wrong frequencies, and that you can swap a system if you have problems. There are also VHF "traveling" channels that don't correspond to any broadcast stations, so you'll want to stick with these if you travel around a lot. The other choice is UHF which has less frequency competition and user-selectable channels.

The first step in determining interference problems is to power up systems without transmitters on and see if any of their RF meters indicate reception. If so, begin cutting off nearby equipment one at a time, especially digital equipment, to see if the RF indicator goes out. You may find that your CD player or reverb unit is causing the problem. Once the culprit is found, you've got a few and/or choices: move the offender or wireless farther away, adjust the mute control (if available) to the point where the RF indicator goes out, or drop adjustable-length antennas down one or two sections from the top. (This acts like a mute control by weakening signal reception.) In the latter two cases, you just want to make sure the adjustment doesn't lose your transmitter signal, too.

Once outside problems are eliminated, it's time to check transmitters one at a time. As each one is cut on, take note if its signal is picked up on more than its own receiver (the RF indicator again). This can be caused by spur frequencies when transmitters are right by the receivers, and will typically disappear when the transmitters are farther away during normal use. If the problem doesn't go away, you have an incompatible system and will have to replace it. This is more common with older systems where frequency filtering may not be adequate. As a result, it is usually better to stick with one manufacturer when combining multiple systems.

Once the transmitters are being properly received, check reception at your maximum working distance from the receivers. If you start getting dropouts, try eliminating them by checking batteries and antenna extension, adjusting antenna angles, making minor mute adjustments, or elevating the receivers. If this doesn't work, you will simply need to move the receivers closer to the transmitters. If you start getting some interference problems at the working distance, you should replicate the checks near the beginning of this section. Be mindful of the possibility for interference from nearby duplicate wireless if you are in a convention or meeting facility, near another church, etc. The unlikelihood of identical frequencies or sheer distance alone is usually sufficient insurance, but it is always wise to plan accordingly for potential problems in these situations.

Gain Settings: Setting proper levels with our gain and volume controls allows us to get a good clear signal without distortion. *Gain* [1] or **trim** usually implies level *into* a device where **volume** or **level** is output *from* a device. Transmitters have a gain control somewhere on the casing, often on the outside as a recessed screw-type adjustment. Otherwise, you'll probably find it in the battery compartment, though a few handheld models have the gain control located on the internal circuit board of the mic. But don't fret about having to make immediate adjustments because, most of the time, gains are set okay from the factory.

Receivers have an audio level control for their outputs, and I normally want this setting all the way up for the strongest signal and lowest noise to my mixer. Most mixers have a gain control and associated peak level indicator on each channel to let you know if the signal is too strong. You'll need to adjust this channel gain to the point where the peak indicator does not illuminate during the loudest signals from the wireless. If your mixer does not have a gain and/or **pad** control on the channel, you will need to back off on the receiver level adjustment if you notice distortion or mixer meters going into the red. (More in Chapter 6.)

The gain setting on the transmitter serves the same purpose. If the level is too strong, the signal will distort. Unlike the mixer settings, I can't make a quick transmitter adjustment once things get going, so I'll want to make sure this is properly set ahead of time. All you need to do is have the mic user speak, sing, or play at their loudest level and see if you notice any distortion in the sound. If not, leave the gain at the factory setting. (If you have an audio level meter or peak indicator on your receiver, it will tell you if the transmitter signal is too strong.) If you do notice distortion and it is not the mixer channel, simply lower the transmitter gain until the audio meter reads normal or the distortion ceases. Check your owner's manual for more specific details.

Equalization: Recommending *EQ* [7] (or tone) settings for your wireless is a little touchy because it is dependent on the sound quality of your speakers and any corrective equalization of the sound system itself. I can offer some appropriate suggestions based on an accurate system, or which should at least get you headed in the right direction for those "I-hope-to-eventually-upgrade" situations. In regard to the following notes, I refer you again to Chapter 6 (mixers) for an in-depth discussion of EQ adjustments including **sweep EQ** which can be essential here.

Handhelds are not much of a problem through a properly tuned system. Prime concern is the proximity effect of unidirectionals. When the user is more than 6" away, you can leave the low end EQ control at the 11:00 to 12:00 position. *Do not boost low end for vocals because it can make the sound muddy or boomy.* As people get closer to the mic, you'll need to decrease the low end more. The same applies for headworn boom mics along with controlling some potential high end "edge" from their smaller condenser elements. If this is too pronounced, you'll need to set the midsweep frequency somewhere between 3kHz and 6.3kHz (around 1:00 to 3:00 on most mixers), and back off its associated mid gain control to the 11:00 or 10:00 position depending on how extensive the "edge" is.

Lavaliers have always been more of a problem due to their off-axis location, requiring more level and EQ adjustment to pick up the voice clearly without feedback. Unidirectional lavaliers tend to sound thinner due to distance rejection and "reverse" proximity effect, and will typically have more feedback problems in the high end from 2kHz to 8kHz. Unfortunately, EQ adjustments to take out this feedback may also diminish critical vocal clarity in the same high end ranges, especially 2.5kHz to 5kHz. This clarity is one of the most important aspects of lavalier performance because, in most rooms, it works in conjunction with the natural projection of ambient low and low-mid sound from the voice itself. Without it the voice sounds muddy from a distance, lacking the supplemental detail necessary for everyone to hear clearly. So EQ accordingly for uni lavaliers without overdoing it and losing your clarity.

Since omnidirectionals don't suffer from gain loss or limited pickup due to rejection, their sonic surplus is in the lower frequencies which can be accentuated by the mic picking up chest resonance. (Put your ear to someone's chest while they're speaking and you'll know what I mean. This is best not performed on strangers.) As a result, we need to decrease specific low and low-mid frequencies which, fortunately, does not affect the clarity range. Depending on the user's vocal tone, I might start by backing off the low end to the 11:00 or 10:00 position to reduce muddiness while taking care not to make the voice sound too thin.

The low-mid problem is around 400Hz to 600Hz which causes a "hollow" muddiness, is most prone to feedback, and which falls within the *room resonance* range of most facilities. This means that the room will actually amplify this range and cause the sound to be even more muddy and reverberant. Reducing these frequencies not only clears up the sound, but diminishes its reverberation in the room. I would start around 600Hz which is typically in the 10:00 to 11:00 range on the midsweep, and reduce the associated mid gain control to the 10:00 or even 9:00 position. You can then re-adjust the midsweep back and forth a little if needed to the point where you get the least feedback and notice the sound being the clearest and most pleasing. Once these ranges are under control, you should have some room to bring up high end if necessary. Most omnis require a little boost on the high EQ, and an extra touch of 2.5kHz in the high-mid may be helpful as well for increasing level on a soft voice if your EQ allows for it.

Obviously, this can be a problem if you don't have midsweep EQ, but I've found a way around this in smaller venues where the ambient voice is more prominent. Without the capability to address specific lower frequencies, we must increase the higher frequencies in an attempt to overcome the predominant lows. To accomplish this with 3-band fixed EQ, first increase the high to around the 3:00 position. Second, if you have a 1kHz mid (notated in the owner's manual specifications), back it off to about 2:00. If it's a 2.5kHz mid, you may need to boost it to 1:00. Finally, adjust the low EQ back one or two notches if the voice still sounds a bit muddy. By just adding supplemental mic level with the natural voice, these settings should help achieve the clarity you need without feedback problems.

Batteries: I once asked a major theatrical engineer if she used rechargeables for her shows. She said, "You don't trust a $10,000,000 show to anything but a fresh alkaline." Though most of you are probably not in a multi-million dollar production, this advice may be appropriate to the importance you place on your task.

Where alkalines will give you at least 8 hours on most newer wireless systems, rechargeables usually last under three hours and they can require following a strict regimen. Rechargeables, except for nickel hydride or lithium, can develop a memory if only partially drained for a routine period of time and then recharged. They will eventually lose their optimum working limit, dying at or before the end of the routine period. To avoid this, you must fully drain the rechargeable after its use before recharging. Also, don't use batteries that don't reach full voltage. Some rechargeable 9V batteries reach under 8 volts max, and some wireless can start to have problems under 8 volts. I've even tested batteries which not only had short operating duration, but whose maximum voltage declined with each recharge.

I always check batteries with a voltage meter before I use them. As I mentioned, the newer wireless systems will typically run 8 hours on a fresh 9V battery, half that long on a used battery down to 8 volts. If you end up with a lot of these, they should still be dependable for a 2-hour dress rehearsal or church service. I prefer that pastors power their wireless on and off as needed to save on batteries, and this is where the *silent on/off* mentioned earlier avoids distracting noises, especially on a preset mixer system.

Another potential problem can be battery contacts. Be aware that batteries can be slightly different in size, so stick to one brand as much as possible. 9V Duracells, for instance, are shorter than most. So if you use a longer battery and then swap to Duracells, the battery contacts may be pushed back a bit too far for good connection. Contacts can also become dirty or oxidized from humidity or perspiration, so clean them periodically with tuner cleaner or alcohol. (Some manufacturers offer gold-plated contacts to reduce this problem.)

This chapter has addressed just about all the wireless considerations and problems I can recall and, hopefully, there won't be too many more popping up. Obviously, attention to detail minimizes the problems, but I still hold to one thought: if you don't need to be unplugged, plug. Wireless are an unparalleled necessity when you need the freedom, but cabled mics present less costs and concerns. Choose wisely. More under **Church Sound** and **Theatrical Sound** in Chapter 12.

5. DOWN TO THE WIRE

CABLES[9]

Now we're concerned with sending our source signals somewhere, so let's briefly touch on the subject of cables and connectors. Always keep in mind that signals flow like water, in one direction. (And for you smart guys who bring up phantom power, I'll say it's like salmon swimming upstream.) We're dealing with two types of signal travel determined by the output and input connections of our equipment — *balanced*[10] and **unbalanced**. Storytime!

> Imagine Mr. Guy Nice walking to the library when he gets followed by a large hissing, snorting bully. Once he reaches the serene environment of his destination, he has brought along a serious and uncontrollable deterrent to bibliophilic harmony. (You can look that up, 'cause I did.) Now imagine Mr. Nice meeting his younger brother at the library, both having been followed by bullies of equal stature and territorial tendencies. At the door, neither goon is willing to give way to the other and they commence in a spirited altercation, leaving the brothers and library patrons inside in perfect peace.

Now stick with me on this. The brothers are your source signals traveling down a cable, the bullies are noise, and the library is your signal destination. The first example is an *unbalanced* cable with noise picked up along its length and no way to keep it from "getting in the door". The second example substitutes a *balanced* cable with an added 'neutral' signal. Once at the destination, the noise introduced to both lines cancels itself out leaving our desired signals undamaged. This is called **common mode rejection**. This is also called a **stretched analogy**.

Unbalancing Act: Unbalanced cables have 2 conductors: a **hot** (+) wire and a **ground** (−) or 'shield' wire. The cable shield is wrapped around the hot wire to keep noise out, but there's a limit to its effectiveness. Noise is at relatively low levels, but gets stronger as it accumulates over a cable's length. **Signal-to-noise** will determine how much of a problem this will cause and what we can get away with. Remember when we talked about source levels and *gain*[1]? A microphone has a low level of around -60dB. If noise accumulates to -70dB over 100' of cable, it will be almost as loud as our signal. As a result, unbalanced high-impedance mics or low-level guitar signals can't be used with long cables. But a +4dB line level from a synthesizer or instrument preamp through the same 100' cable would yield a 74dB signal-to-noise difference which can effectively mask noise. Such lines, therefore, could feasibly employ a long run except for one other possibility — *ground loops*[11].

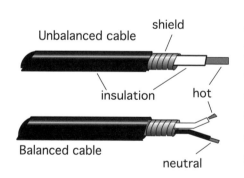

No, ground loops are not a new high fiber cereal. They are hums caused by the signal cable ground of one *AC-powered* unit connected to another, more specifically when they're plugged into different AC wall circuits. So we would have to break the signal ground somehow to eliminate our final connection problem, and you can't do it with an unbalanced line because it will cut your audio. The good news is that balanced lines can help eliminate both noise and ground loops.

Balancing Act: Balanced cables have 3 conductors as illustrated: a **hot** (+), a **neutral** (−), and a **ground**. The hot and neutral carry the actual signal, so the ground can be cut at one end to eliminate a ground loop if one appears. The rule is to cut it at the output, or sending, connector of a device. Without even saying, "Abracadabra", all your noise problems will disappear and everyone will be in awe of your power. There have been rare occasions, though, when I was waiting for the applause and suddenly realized that the noise was still there. This could indicate a problem with equipment, incompatible chassis ground designs, or inherent noise in the source or AC lines. Beginning at sources, start cutting off or unplugging things one at a time and possibly switching AC circuits to track this one down.

Another cute trick is eliminating a ground loop from an unbalanced output. As long as your destination is a balanced input, a cable can be made that connects the *hot* and *ground* of the output unit to the *hot* and *neutral* of the destination input with the same results because the ground of the input is not connected. More applause!

Direct Box: Unbalanced lines can be changed to balanced with a unit called a ***direct box***[6]. This is a $10 balancing transformer that sells for $40 because musicians are suckers. It normally offers two 1/4" phone jacks and an XLR connector. Plug the instrument into one 1/4", run a patch cable from the other to the instrument amp (if applicable), and a mic line from the XLR to the mixer. Most also have a ground lift switch to break a ground loop. A direct box is especially necessary with low level sources such as bass or guitar, but should be used on any unbalanced sources having to traverse more than 30' of cable.

These connections are all used for mic and line sources, and require shielded cables. You'll also find a great deal of these in a single convenient package called a **snake** cable for running long distances. Speakers require larger gauge cables with side by side wiring. I'll elaborate on them later.

CONNECTORS

There are only a few standard connectors used in audio, so I'll give a brief description and their wiring configurations:

1/4" phone plug: the most common, this is a 2-conductor connector; tip=hot, sleeve=ground.

1/4" TRS phone plug: this is a 3-conductor version with **T**ip, **R**ing, and **S**leeve connections; ring=neutral.
(Also used for stereo plugs with Left, Right, and ground connections as used for headphones.
Another configuration for *inserts*[12] will be discussed in the Mixer section.)

RCA phono plug: hi-fi style connector; tip=hot, sleeve=ground.

XLR male plug: the most popular 3-conductor connector, the male version connects to inputs; three numbered pins are wired to an international standard: 1=ground, 2=hot, 3=neutral.

XLR female plug: the female version commonly connects to outputs, same pin standard as male. (Some manufacturers have previously designed equipment with XLRs wired Pin 2=*neutral* and Pin 3=*hot*. Talk about rebels! Check the manuals of older gear and consider having the equipment connector wiring corrected if not standard.)

I'd also like to make note of a unique *solderless* XLR plug made by Alcatel. You need only strip the overall wire insulation, and the connector provides excellent strain relief while making connection to the individual wires with contact pins (similar to a telephone wiring panel) when the connector base is tightened. I've found them extremely reliable and especially convenient for reversing polarity and lifting grounds on the fly, though they should be limited to 24 or 22 gauge cable. (Alcatel even got cute and made the internal body blue for XLR male and pink for XLR female. Give 'em a hand for originality and cosmetics.)

One more thing — whenever I start having signal problems, static, a drop in levels, no audio, whatever, the first thing to check is connectors and cables. It can be as simple as dirty contacts or a broken wire either at the solder connections or at the stress point of the cable where it exits the connector. Nothing that a soldering iron or a little contact cleaner can't handle. Regular checks along with some routine unplugging and plugging to clean contacts won't hurt either. And it's a lot easier than fielding the complaints later.

6. BASIC PLUMBING 101

MIXERS

Now we get to the heart of the whole operation. The mixer will control almost everything from here on out and, consequently, is the most complex piece to use. All mixers are basically the same, just some have more features or higher quality components than others. The bigger a mixer is, the more critical its circuit design to keep accumulated electronic noise at a minimum. A real cause for confusion is the terminology. *Nobody* can seem to get together on what to call stuff! One man's gain is another man's trim, one man's aux is another man's send. I think this probably dates back to that Tower of Babel thing. Anyway, we'll cover some audio semantics along the way.

There are as many mixer designs as there are guitarists' egos, and I'm not inclined to elaborate on either one. You will find the smaller units are usually box-style **powered mixers** with 4 to 8 channels within $1000 or console-style with 8 to 16 channels within $2000, all with the amplifier(s) built-in. **Unpowered mixers** from 8 to 40 channels can run from under $500 to $10,000 or more.

First priority in choosing a mixer is how many sources you must accommodate. Always get a few extra channels for surprise needs. Next priority is how many aux sends you will need for stage monitors, effects, recording feeds, etc. (I recommend at least four in most situations.) Any other considerations will usually be based on what you can afford. This will determine how many bells and whistles you can reap in the process. Let's find out about some basic bells first.

EVERYTHING *AND* THE KITCHEN SINK

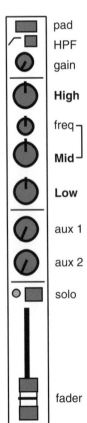

"Do you know what all those knobs do?" If I had a nickel for every time I was asked that question, I wouldn't be writing this book. Yes I do, and it's not that hard. Most of what you need to know is what one channel strip does. The rest just do the same thing for other sources. And each channel works just like your kitchen sink! Follow me on a pipe dream . . .

Gain[1] – Check out the valve on one of your pipes under the sink. This valve controls the flow of water into the line. By comparison, a **gain**, **trim**, or **attenuation** knob at the top of a mixer channel controls the source level into the channel, allowing us to get good pressure without bursting anything.

Fader – Note the faucet on top of the sink; this controls the amount you wish to use from the line. So does the fader, or volume knob, on a mixer.

Auxes[13] – Now let's say we have an icemaker in the fridge. We hook a small tap and valve off the pipe under the sink and feed the hose over to the icemaker. We've just employed an auxiliary line to feed another device, just as a channel can feed to effects or stage monitors. Such channel controls may be called **aux**, **effect**, **send**, **monitor**, **foldback**, or **cue**.

EQ[7] – Finally, we'll hook up an activated charcoal filter on the line to remove impurities from the water. Likewise, the channel **equalizer** (tone control) is a filter to control tonal characteristics.

That's all the major channel controls. For each type of level control on each channel, there will usually be a corresponding master control such as Aux 1 master, Effect Send master, Main fader, etc. The whistles will determine our flexibility in choosing how auxes are affected by other things on the channel, where we want to send our channel outputs, EQ control, etc.

INPUT STAGE

Finally, we get back to that part about sources and levels in the beginning. The proper mixer will provide the balanced and unbalanced input connections needed for your sources. Then the signal goes straight to the *gain*[1] control where we can accommodate all those great variations in dB levels. We'll bring up the gain control for those low level mic signals, and bring it down for those hot keyboard signals.

How do we know when the setting is right? Most mixers have a channel peak LED that will light up red when the signal is too hot and might distort or damage something. While the source is playing (or singing) its loudest, bring up the gain until you see red. Then drop it back a notch or so and you're set. What if it's all the way down and you still see red? This may occur with hot signals like bass drum or line levels, so some mixers have a gain **pad** switch that will drop the level another 20dB, giving you more range to make your adjustment. If the mixer has channel **PFL** or **Solo** switches (see "Downtown"), they will typically route channel level to an indicated master meter for more precise display. Then simply adjust gain for an average "0" meter reading. Check the owner's manual for specific details.

There will usually be *phantom power*[3] switching available somewhere, either as a global switch or on individual channels. This cuts on a 24 to 48 volt DC supply to the balanced XLR inputs for those condenser mics we spoke about. The (+) voltage travels down the hot *and* neutral wire, and the (–) voltage travels through the ground shield. A global phantom power will not affect dynamic mics, but *can be shorted by an unbalanced XLR cable with pin 1 jumped to pin 2 or 3*. Phantom power may affect some instrument preamps, but a direct box should eliminate the problem.

Other channel features on higher line mixers are **HPF** (**H**igh **P**ass **F**ilter) switches to reduce bass frequencies, and *phase reverse*[14] which can occasionally help with feedback or balanced sources that are wired up backwards. I'll talk more about this when we get into applications where all these tidbits start coming together. (Plus, it's 2AM in the morning and I think *my* phase is a little reversed.)

PRE/POST AUXES[13]

Let's go back to our icemaker hookup. Tapped off the pipe under the sink, it will obviously be controlled by the input valve. It will not be affected by the faucet, therefore we'll call it 'pre-faucet'. If we could hook it up after the faucet, we would call it post-faucet and it *would* be affected. Likewise, if the tap is before the charcoal filter, it is pre-filter and impurities will not be removed from the icemaker line. If connected post-filter, it will get filtered water.

The same goes for channel auxes. They can be tapped off the circuit **pre** or **post EQ**, and **pre** or **post fader**. (The owner's manual should illustrate which ones are which in a simple 'map' called the **block diagram**.) The fancier mixers will often include pre/post aux switches so you'll have a choice. Generally speaking, stage monitor feeds are pre-fader auxes. This is so changes you make in fader level for the room sound won't alter monitor levels or cause potential feedback. However, I prefer post-fader auxes for most sources in church services since, unlike the typical concert, performers may be changing from week to week. Rather than constantly altering pre-fader monitor settings, it can simply be easier having good monitor levels adjust appropriately with my fader moves. If a singer is louder then last week's, I bring them down in the house and they drop proportionately in the monitors. Same in reverse for a soft singer. As a result, balancing the house sound simultaneously balances the monitors.

Post-fader is also preferred for accompaniment soundtracks. If the song is a bit too soft in the beginning, a fader increase for the congregation reflects in the monitors so performers can cue off the music better. If it's a live performance track that needs to be faded in or out, this will also fade the monitor feed. (A pre-fader aux would allow the music to continue blasting through the monitors after the house sound is faded.)

To provide flexibility in these instances, it is best when a mixer has pre/post switching on *every* channel for aux singles or pairs. This allows me to select the primary vocal leader and instrument channels for pre-fader monitors as needed. Though some auxes are made pre-channel EQ, I prefer post-EQ so that any necessary tonal adjustments will be reflected in the monitors, too. Effects feeds are post-EQ/post-fader auxes to allow the effects you add to follow the original signal in tone and balance.

EQUALIZERS[7]

Many people use EQ like Wizard air freshener. Something stinks, so they start adding stuff to try to cover it up. You can find these people by looking at their EQ knobs; all the notches will be pointing to the right side. If something stinks in my house, my solution is to get rid of the problem first. (Then I have to buy all new socks!)

When you're listening to a sound, don't think about what it's missing. Think first about what it's got too much of. This was the basis for my previous drum and wireless mic EQ suggestions. If a drum or mic sounds muddy, most people would probably try to cover it up with an abundance of high EQ. This creates frequency peaks that are harsh and more prone to feedback. Better to eliminate the muddiness first, then add subtle amounts of high end if needed. Don't be a "Mr. Wizard"! Use both sides of the EQ knobs. Before we start turning knobs, however, let's find out what we're controlling when we do.

Hertz: Tonal frequencies are designated in **Hertz (Hz)**, or cycles per second. The audible range is 20Hz to 20,000Hz (20kHz=kiloHertz). Below is a graph describing the different frequency ranges and their positive and negative characteristics. (I hope you appreciate the brilliant terminology.) This should be a valuable aid in learning how to pinpoint and control your equalization.

+	Demolition? Subsonic	Tight kick Boominess	Fullness Muddiness	Warmth Hollowness	Definition Harshness	Clarity Piercing	Brightness Edgy/whistley	Brilliance Sibilance
−	L	O	W	M	I	D	H	I	G	H
	20Hz	40Hz	70Hz	200Hz	500Hz	2kHz	5kHz	10kHz	20kHz

From the preceding graph, you can note particular sonic characteristics you need to control and adjust accordingly. Following are some more tips and information:

55–70Hz:	The chest-resonant range where you feel tight kick. Too much is boomy and wastes watts.
100–250Hz:	There are usually muddy problems to take out here, but can also be used to add fullness to a "midrangy" sound.
300–500Hz:	Adds warmth to a thin sound. Too much causes a hollow resonance which can be accentuated by large rooms.
500–2kHz:	Critical tone for most acoustic sources. Cut if sound is harsh or "nasally."
2kHz–5kHz:	Guitar edge, drum attack, vocal presence, etc. Ear's most sensitive range, so don't overdo it. Cut if sound is piercing.
5kHz–10kHz:	Can add brightness, but too much is prone to a brittle or whistley sound. Hiss is typically above 8k.
10kHz–15kHz:	Cuts excessive sibilance, or adds sweet-sounding highs on vocals, cymbals, string instruments, etc.

EQ Features: Your stereo hi-fi probably has a bass and treble control. This would be **2-band fixed EQ**. The same applies to basic mixers. These are typically **shelving** controls, boosting (to the right) or cutting (to the left) a broad "shelf" of frequencies at 100Hz and below for bass and 10kHz and above for treble. Each notch is a subtle change in the frequency level and straight up (or 12:00) is **flat**, or no change. Some units also have a mid control centered at around 1kHz to 2kHz. It's called a **peak & dip** control because the EQ curve would be represented by a boosted "hill" or cut "hole" shape centered around the set frequency. So, what if we want to change 500Hz? What if there's *feedback*[4] at 5kHz? We've got a little bit of a problem because our midrange control isn't fixed at those points.

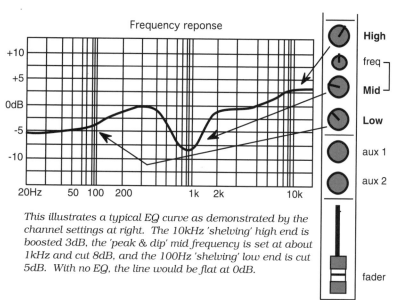

This illustrates a typical EQ curve as demonstrated by the channel settings at right. The 10kHz 'shelving' high end is boosted 3dB, the 'peak & dip' mid frequency is set at about 1kHz and cut 8dB, and the 100Hz 'shelving' low end is cut 5dB. With no EQ, the line would be flat at 0dB.

Enter **sweep EQ**. In addition to our midrange control knob, there is an adjacent *frequency* knob that allows us to vary a whole range of mid frequencies. Now our midrange isn't limited to a fixed point, but will sweep from say 200Hz to 5kHz. Now I can set it at 5kHz and cut down the mid control to get rid of that feedback. Even if I've got feedback I can't pinpoint, the sweep will help find it. I just set the mid control at about the 10:00 position and rotate the corresponding frequency knob until I hear the feedback dip or stop. The same can be done for a muddy sound. Rotate frequency until the mud is gone. Then fine adjust the mid control to take out only as much as you need to. Frequency found. Problem precluded.

This EQ configuration would be called **3-band w/sweep mid**. A better board might have a sweep on all three controls. Add a **"Q"** (width) adjustment and you get **parametric EQ** where you can set how broad a range of frequencies are affected by each control. The better the EQ, the more flexibility and ear training you'll get.

Tone Tips: Now that you understand something about EQ, it's safe to assume you should start making major adjustments to all your sources. Right? WRONG, bandwidth breath! A speaker system with accurate response will eliminate the need for excessive tonal adjustments. Sources such as CDs, *quality* cassettes, keyboards, properly mic'ed acoustic instruments, and vocals should require little or no EQ. Some sources that usually require more conscientious adjustment are close-mic'ed drums and piano, instrument pickups run direct, and condensers used for choir, podium, and wireless lavaliers (primarily to control feedback points). Some specific techniques will be touched on in Chapter 11.

BUSSES

Just as the term seems to imply, **busses** are the lines that transport our channels 'downtown' to the master section. If there is only one buss line running, you will only have a volume control on the channel. If there are two buss (or stereo) lines, you will also have a *pan*[15] control which can be adjusted to send the channel to the Left or Right output or any combination of the two. If there are more than two buss lines, there will be additional **assignment switches** to select which pair(s) you wish to use. The pan will again be adjusted to send to the odd or even-numbered output. There are usually 4 or 8 assignable busses, and several reasons for them. One is to feed multitrack recorders. For example, with 8 buss outputs on a mixer, I can connect directly to all inputs of an 8-track studio recorder. Then I can send any mixer channel to any track I want to record on by just assigning the appropriate buss. In the same way, I can also send various channels out to different amps and speakers in a room if I wish.

Another purpose is called **channel grouping**. It's the reason busses are also called *groups*[16], and all these groups have the capability of being routed to main outputs that will feed your speakers. There are many times when it's nice to have a single volume control for a whole bunch of specific channels. For instance, in the case of multiple drum channels, I can assign them all to the same group. Then if I wish to control the drum level, I can simply adjust that group's master fader instead of six channel faders at once. (I wouldn't want to strain myself.) I can assign different groups for multiple channels of vocals, guitars, keyboards, etc.

DOWNTOWN

In the master section we have a few extra inputs, master controls for everything coming off the channels, level meters, and main, group, and aux outputs. Main outputs go to the speaker amplifiers and any stereo recorders, aux outputs go to effects or stage monitor amplifiers, and group outputs can go to a multitrack recorder (if any). Some larger live consoles also have **matrix** outputs. These are simply 'auxes' for the group outputs rather than the channels. They can be used if you wish to send a simple group mix to another location.

Headphone outputs and studio control room feeds on recording consoles will allow you to monitor various outputs as well as individual channels if special **Solo** buttons are provided. As the name suggests, Solo will send one selected item alone to the headphones for your scrutiny. Such buttons may also be called **Cue** and **PFL** (pre-fader listen), or **AFL** (after-fader listen) which is the same as Solo. The difference is that Cue or PFL will allow you to monitor a source with its fader level off while Solo or AFL reflects actual fader settings and stereo pan positions. For the most part, PFL is preferred for live sound and AFL for recording. Some dual-purpose mixers will allow you to switch between both.

The extra inputs will be *effects* or *stereo returns*[17]. They're actually the same as other channels except that they lack many of the features such as balanced inputs, gains, EQ, or auxes. You will need to refer to specific mixers as to what they offer in their master package.

Levels: The most important point I can make here is not to overdrive your mixer outputs. Your meters will let you know what's going on. Set all your master levels at *nominal*[2] which is usually represented by a "0" or thick mark on most controls. If in doubt, set master faders at two-thirds and knobs at halfway. Adjust individual channel levels as needed. Meters should hit at 0dB to +3dB maximum. If your system still isn't loud enough, your equipment levels are mismatched or you need additional amps and speakers. More later in the Amplifier section.

RECORDING MIXERS

The things that make recording most different from live sound are the controlled environment, a conceptual approach to the recording process (covered in Chapter 11), and the mixer. While all mixers have essentially the same features, one thing sets recording mixers apart — **tape returns**. In live PA, we are dealing with a single-stage process. The sources come into the mixer and are sent out to the speaker system. In multitrack recording, it's a two-stage process. Sources come into the mixer and out to a recorder, then back from the recorder to the mixer tape returns which feed the monitoring system. These returns are additional channels that allow us to independently monitor tape tracks during recording or playback while the main channels are being used to send sources to the recorder, and without affecting actual recording levels. Most recording consoles are 'inline' designs with dual inputs and controls, for a channel and a tape return, on each channel strip. A special switch can "flip" the tape outputs from the returns over to the main channels when it's time to mix everything down to stereo.

Other standard features on a recording mixer are **direct outputs** for sending individual channels to tape, separate stereo studio and control room outputs, a talkback mic to studio or tape, and stereo 2-track returns for the mixdown deck. Refer to specific manuals for hookup and available features.

Digital Mixing (see Digital Domains, p. 40): Yamaha was the first to introduce affordable digital mixers like the Promix 01, 02R, and 03D in the mid - '90s, establishing a new precedent in mixing technology. These were followed several years later by offerings from Ramsa, Tascam, Mackie, and others. In the future, we will see most (if not all) mixers resorting to digital technology due to the numerous advantages including *full parametric* EQ on each channel, *motorized* moving faders, built-in effects and signal processors, automated mixing and recall of complete mixer settings, and flexible digital routing of inputs and outputs. They also allow direct integration with other digital devices like recorders, processors, and related computer software as they become available.

With smaller mixers (including analog models), you may find a need for additional inputs and/or routing of signals and equipment, especially in the studio. Though digital mixers usually offer these expandable options on-board, **patchbays** and **mic preamps** are external devices that can expand on the capabilities of almost any mixer system.

Patchbays: As if you don't have enough connections already, let's add a few hundred more! It can actually make some things easier in a fixed installation, and you've already gone too far to turn back now. So when there are just too many input and output connections spread out all over the studio and behind your equipment, why not bring them all to one central, accessible spot — the patchbay.

All the desired gear hooks into the back of the patchbay, and can be designated with labels (or freehand scribblings for the meticulous) on the front. Whenever something needs to be connected to something else, we plug patch cords in the front from designated outputs to selected inputs. There are usually two rows of 16 to 24 connections with a selection of RCA or balanced and unbalanced phone connectors available.

A **normalled** patchbay means it can already have over/under connections made for you. If, for example, an output like an aux send is hooked to a rear connection on the top row and an effects input is hooked up directly under it, the normalled circuit has already connected them so you don't need a patch cable. However, if you plug a patch cable into the front jack of either one, it disconnects them so they can be routed elsewhere. There's also **half-normalled** where only one of the jacks will cause a disconnect, and **parallel-normalled** where neither one will. This just makes it possible to expand and tailor a complex system to your specific needs.

Mic Preamps: These are 'mini-mixers' that don't mix! Go figure. That's because they are basic balanced mic inputs, each with a separate direct output. Simple features include gain, phantom power, some kind of level or peak indication, and maybe phase reverse. No EQ, no auxes, no busses, no downtown. This lack of additional circuitry makes for high quality 'straightline' design. They're available in solid state and tube circuit versions offering one to eight preamps in a single unit.

In addition to their studio appeal, they can be useful in live remote recording. Three 8-channel mic preamps like the Presonus M80 or Grace Designs 801 offer 24 inputs and outputs for 24-track recording in a few spaces of an equipment rack. Some preamps now offer analog-to-digital conversion for direct digital input into today's multitracks.

PROCESSOR CONNECTIONS

The next few chapters will be devoted to effects and signal processors that aren't built-in, so let's talk about how these are connected to the mixer. We'll discuss two types of hookups — **direct** and **sidechain**.

Direct: Signal processors include units such as equalizers, compressors, noise gates, noise reduction, etc. The purpose of these is to process the whole signal to achieve the desired result. One way of doing this is to plug the source straight into a compatible device, then out of the device to wherever you're going. Another method is using mixer *inserts*[12].

Inserts are **send and return** connections that are available at several points along the mixer's signal path. They will usually be on every channel, allowing processors to be easily hooked to individual sources. They can also be on groups or main outputs so you can process several things or everything at once.

Most inserts use a **1/4" TRS** phone connection, but not for a balanced function as we learned in the Input stage. Though configuration may vary, the Tip is usually the return from the processor and the **R**ing is the send to it. The **S**leeve is the common ground as always. When the plug of an **insert cable** is pushed into the insert, it automatically disconnects the mixer circuit at that point so the signal has to go through the processor and back. The other end of the insert cable has two separate connectors corresponding to the send and return; these plug into the processor input and output respectively. (If you're plugged in with processor on and no signal is flowing, you probably just have the connections backwards.)

If your mixer manual indicates the insert Ring is a send, you can also plug a mono 1/4" connection in halfway to get a pre-fader direct out without disconnecting the internal jumper of the insert jack. This allows you to feed the line level signal of the inserts to multichannel recording or monitoring systems without affecting your mixer channel operation.

Side-Chain: An effect such as reverb or echo, on the other hand, is an embellishment to the original signal. It doesn't need to be processing the whole signal, just added to it. Accordingly, it is normally connected to an *aux*[13] output which sends its side signal to the effect input, then the effect output is patched to an *effects return*[17] to be added to the mix. Since most channels would have control to this aux output, the effect can be added to any one of them. Also, a regular channel can be used as an effects return if you need the added features of EQ, pan, or monitor sends for the effect. Just don't loop an effect through itself by inadvertently bringing up its aux send on its own return channel.

Another point is that effects have a **balance** or **mix** control. This determines how much original signal is mixed in with the effect. In a mixer side-chain hookup, we already have original signal passing straight through the mixer so we don't want it coming through the effects unit, too. So set the mix control *all* the way to "wet," "effect," 100%, whatever your unit calls it. (That terminology thing, again.) If you choose to run a source directly through an effects unit or patch through an insert connection, you'll need to adjust the mix control for the desired blend of original and effected signal.

7. CAUSE & EFFECT

Trying to discuss the current state of effects devices is like trying to track the federal deficit — five minutes later, you're out of touch and it's out of sight! Frankly, I don't relish my whole life becoming a successive parade of new product learning curves. Give me at least a few meager minutes for coffee and Headline News.

Seriously, it is truly amazing the quality and flexibility of today's digital effects. But to be practical and avoid a section rivaling Tolstoy's *War and Peace*, let me just give you a few meager minutes of basic descriptions and tips on the more common ones.

DELAY[18]

This is considered a single repeat of an original signal, with the delay time designated in milliseconds. 10–50ms can fatten up a vocal, 50–100ms gives the slapback effect of small to medium rooms, and 100–250ms simulates larger room delays. Longer times are not very natural short of the Grand Canyon, and would be used primarily for special effects.

In recording, I sometimes like to use a good delay to stereo image a mono source. Just pan the original sound to one side, and pan an effect unit's 10-20ms delayed return of the source to the other. You might notice something unusual, though. If they're both set to the same meter levels, the original side still sounds louder. This is called the **Haas effect**[19]. If a separate delayed signal is within 40ms of the original, the sound will be perceived as coming primarily from the direction of the first signal. It fools your ears. We'll find out later that the Haas effect has a very useful purpose in large room sound system setups.

ECHO

Delay with decaying repeats. Adjustments of **feedback** or **regeneration**, as it is called, is usually in percentages. I only use 15–25% for smooth 200ms echoes with three to four repeats. I also prefer using quarter-note triplet echoes in music, because they will be more noticeable between the beats without overdoing the echo level. (If you don't understand triplets, swallow your pride and ask a musician to explain it.)

REVERB[20]

Reverb is very short echoes, or multiple reflections, so numerous that they create a dense and continuous effect that gradually decays. Natural reverb times for a good concert hall are 1.5 to 2.5 seconds long. A **pre-delay** setting, which simulates the wall reflection preceding reverberation, can be set for 50–100ms to give the reverb more depth and slightly distance it from the original signal for clarity.

There are different types of reverbs to simulate various room characteristics, namely **hall**, **chamber**, and **room**. Another more synthetic type is **plate**, a bright sounding effect simulating the large metal plate reverbs of yesteryear, and **gated** (or **reverse**) reverb with an abrupt cutoff of the decay as if shut down by a noise gate. This is very popular on snare drum, and short versions make for an interesting 'dense delay' effect. In popular music production, I normally reduce the bass frequencies in reverb to avoid smearing the low end of the mix.

MODULATED EFFECTS

Chorus is a lush effect that delays and modulates a pitch around the original note. I don't favor it much on vocals, but it's really nice on instruments where it adds color and fullness. It can give 6-string guitar a sound similar to a 12-string. **Flange** (I call it chorus with an attitude) is a short-delay chorus regenerated through itself to produce a more radical and hollow sounding effect. **Leslie simulation** is another chorus variation based on the Doppler effect of the Leslie rotating speakers used with the classic Hammond organs. A unique feature is the switched and gradual speeding up and slowing down of the modulation to mimic the motorized action of a Leslie.

PITCH SHIFT

This one is pretty self-explanatory. It changes the pitch of a note to a selected interval which stays constant, unlike chorus which modulates around the note. Coarse adjustment is in half-step note (semi-tone) increments and fine adjustments are in percentages of a half-step. With a fine adjustment of 10–15%, you get an effect similar to chorus but cleaner, especially for vocal, since it isn't waving around. Coarse adjustment on vocal tends to get you into a higher "munchkin" or lower "demonic" -sounding effect.

I call this "stupid" pitch shift, because we also have **intelligent pitch shift**, or **harmonizing**, which goes a step further. You can select a root key and a musical scale, or mode, and the pitch will follow musical notes in specific harmony intervals allowing you to sing or play harmony with yourself! Units which have offered this include the Eventide Harmonizers, Yamaha SPX990, and Digitech Vocalizers. In addition, there are high-quality **intonation processors** like the Antares ATR-1 that will correct pitch in real time. It's getting to the point where, if you can't carry a tune in a bucket, you can dump it from an intonation processor.

There are many other special effects such as distortion, ring modulation, phasing, wah wah, auto-panning, sampling, multitap echo, et-et-et-etcetera. There's a bazillion things you can do with these and combinations of effects that will require your own dedicated experimentation. I guess this is something like bungee jumping. It may be intimidating at first, but the results can be exhilarating. Or they may scare the begeebees out of you. (Imagine that, I've sunk to "bazillion" and "begeebees" in the same paragraph!)

8. SIGNAL CORPS

TO *BBE* OR NOT TO *BBE* . . .

Signal processing, if you'll remember, is a direct hookup that affects the whole signal. It can provide tremendous benefits, but you rarely get something for nothing (unless you're a politician). Anytime you process something, you get a little farther from its natural state. Maybe its natural state sounds like garbage so you have nothing to lose. But if it sounds decent, the trick is to get it through the system with as little mangling as possible. I've actually had recording clients come into the studio with only one concern on their minds — how many graphic equalizers I had. "Sure, I do all my critical recording on a 1978 Sanyo boombox, and my 22 graphics make it sound just like a CD!" Shoot me now.

Signal processors should never be a crutch for poor engineering or system design. Try a different mic, better speakers, improved mixer EQ technique, milk it for all it's worth before you patch in another device. When it *is* time, here are some of your choices . . .

AURAL ENHANCERS

Since I so cleverly used **BBE** in the header to make a point, I figured I should probably elaborate. This is an economical sonic processor that can improve the clarity and dimension of a mix, a trait called 'transparency' where the instruments and vocals stand out more clearly. With optimum equipment and current digital technology, you should be able to achieve this without a BBE, but it sure helped me through a lot of analog recording projects with some great results. As with most processors, just don't overdo it!

Another enhancement processor is the **aural exciter**. This one adds narrowband high harmonics for a sweet 'breathy' high end, particularly for vocals. It uses harmonic distortion to achieve the effect, so I would recommend using it on specific individual sources rather than on a whole mix.

GRAPHIC EQ

A professional graphic equalizer breaks down the frequencies we studied into 15 to 31 separate controls, allowing us to adjust any or all of them individually. Graphics are used in live sound to correct for room acoustics and speaker response deficiencies, and there are some easy clues as to when a system is well-tuned: a CD should sound perfect played through the system with its channel EQ set to flat, and so should a good vocal mic from 6-12". (If closer, the bassy proximity effect of most unidirectional mics necessitates cutting back the low channel EQ.)

Graphics include a level control for maintaining *nominal*[2] gain. Once an EQ is set, hit the Bypass switch to see if the perceived level changes due to your EQ settings. If it does, adjust the level control so it's equal when you switch back and forth. This is also called **unity gain**, maintaining proper levels through the system without loss or undue excess.

Since room and speaker anomalies are so numerous, no one can tell you how to set a graphic. I *have* found that many large rooms have problems around 100Hz and 400Hz, and horns may need control around 2–4kHz to smooth out peaks. Feedback frequencies also need to be addressed. If you want to get more accurate settings, read on.

Realtime Analyzer: This is a device designed to help you determine accurate response for your speakers. It's not a signal processor, but it needs mentioning here since it will help you set up a graphic equalizer. This unit has a broad LED or meter readout corresponding to all the frequencies of the graphic, a calibrated microphone for reading frequencies, and a **pink noise** generator. Pink noise is all frequencies produced simultaneously and sounds like what it implies — noise. Like a roomful of people all talking at the same time. Or maybe just your mother-in-law.

There's a tactic to using an analyzer. A good studio monitor has *flat* [21] (accurate) response as measured within a set distance. Add another speaker and you get more bass from 'coupling'. Move farther away and you lose high end from absorption in the air. Therefore, if I analyze *multiple* stacks of PA speakers from too great a distance, I'll set the EQ for too much highs and not enough bass. (Think about it, or take my word for it.)

To balance things out, I place the analyzer mic within 30' in front of *one* speaker or stack. With all EQ set to flat, pink noise is run into a channel and brought up through the speakers to an average expected performance volume. Now the pink noise, mixer, and amps constitute a flat signal. Any discrepancies read by the analyzer can, for all practical purposes, be attributed to the speakers and/or room.

Mic sensitivity is set on the analyzer to a point where the meter levels are equally distributed on either side of the center line. Individual graphic frequencies are then adjusted up or down opposite the analyzer, bringing the meters as close to a flat center line as possible. This corrects speaker response and compensates for major room resonances.

Afterwards, I'll analyze stage monitors at close range, then check for any consistent feedback problems by bringing up all the mics and fine tuning graphics accordingly. As you can guess, an RTA can be a good investment and a great aid in developing a "Golden Ear". Units start at around $400.

COMPRESSOR/LIMITER

You're running sound when suddenly, the singer hits a high note that does a light show on your meters and turns your tweeters into confetti. You have three choices: shoot the singer, take up needlepoint, or add another set of helping hands — the compressor/limiter.

Compression gently controls level where **limiting** aggressively stops it. The **ratio** control determines which is occurring. A 1:1 ratio setting means for every 1dB of signal coming in, 1dB is getting out — no change, no compression. A 4:1 ratio means that for every 4dB of signal coming in, only 1dB is getting out — 75% compression, or one-fourth the peak we would have gotten otherwise. Anything greater than 10:1 is considered limiting. A **threshold** control sets the max level where the compressor should cut in, and our new hands are ready to start grabbing peaks. Other controls include input and output to match unity gain, and **attack** and **release** to adjust reaction time and duration. Check manuals for more details.

I rarely use compression on sources other than vocals because I like to maintain natural dynamics, and many instrument peaks are due to resonant frequencies which I can control with EQ. Always use such processing sparingly and on individual sources for best results. I wouldn't recommend using a compressor on a total recording mixdown unless it's a quality tube model, and only then at a mild 2:1 ratio. (Tubes are kinder and gentler.)

Limiting is used more for protection. It can be applied to main or monitor mixer outputs to avoid overdriving amplifiers and speakers. The threshold is set so that limiting starts just prior to amplifier clipping (overload). Where compression uses a more gradual response called "soft knee" (representing a more rounded threshold curve), limiting uses a "hard knee" peak response to avoid squashing the sound prior to the threshold. The Behringer Composer and DBX compressors both have peak limiting capabilities to name a few, and many amps have some form of clip-limiting built in. I recommend using it if it's available.

NOISE GATE[8]

A noise gate is an automatic on/off switch. Again you have a **threshold**, but this one is set at a minimum level where the gate should cut in. When used on a mic channel, a low or absent signal triggers the gate to cut off the mic so nothing else bleeds through.

A simple gate is generally found on most compressor/limiters. More complex dedicated units will have adjustable **attack**, **hold**, **decay**, or **rate** controlling opening and closing duration, as well as **floor** or **range** to adjust the gate so that it never fully closes. A slow attack delays opening so that you could eliminate a problem at the start of a sound. A slow decay or rate will avoid noticeable cutoff of a gradually decaying sound like cymbals.

Another important processor is the **electronic crossover**. This requires an understanding of amplification and speaker components, so I choose to cover this in the Speaker section. You got a problem with that?

I might also mention the resurgence of **tube processors** in recent years. With the stark reality of digital recording, tubes are in greater demand for the warmth and "harmonic smoothing" they can offer. It's similar to the visual difference between video and film where film can have a softer, more pleasing look in many cases. Tube equipment like mic preamps, compressors, and EQs cost more than solid state and, if not a necessity, can at least offer an excellent variation from solid state processing where desired. (Interestingly enough, I've found high-resolution digital mixers and processors offering similar advantages due to the smoothness of the waveform and the absence of phase shift and distortion associated with analog mixer and equipment integration.)

9. POWER TOOLS

NO PAIN, NO GAIN

This is the macho section, dealing with devices of sheer brute force. . . heavy current draw. . . massive gain. . . shattered speakers. . . Tim Allen, eat your heart out! Amplifiers take our measly signals from the mixer and boost them enough to move speakers and, hopefully, our sense of good taste. Pro amps can provide power of 100 watts to 2,000 watts or more. Since these are the most powerful electronic devices we will be using, they possess the potential for doing the most damage. We want the right amp for our application and enough power for our needs without overloading anything along the way.

So Watt! So how much wattage is enough? Loose answers are based on several factors: "How many vocals/instruments do I have? Am I amplifying bass or drums? What are the capabilities of my speakers? How large is the area I need to cover?" (See, now I'm talking to myself.)

Let me just throw you some rough ideas in this area. Bare minimum I need is about 200 watts total, or 100 watts per channel stereo for nearfield monitors in a small studio. In live sound, one watt per person room capacity is a reasonable starting point, especially for churches and small performance venues. The same 200 watts should cover minimal PA needs for up to 200 people, moderate volume, 6-8 channels of vocals and light rhythm instruments (guitar, keyboard, kazoo, spoons, etc.). Increase total wattage proportionately to room and audience size.

For more powerful club and concert levels, 2 or more watts per person should be available along with speakers suited to the task. With live drums and bass running through the system, I recommend a minimum of around 800-1000 watts for smaller rooms. You can rarely have too much power, so our budgets will keep us within a practical range.

Sound Pressure: Now we need to understand how we hear these wattage differences. This can also be represented by dBs relative to the way we hear sound, and is called **SPL**[22] or **sound pressure level**. Where only about 10% of people can hear a 1dB change in level, around 50% of people can hear a 2dB change, and just about anybody can hear a 3dB change. Now the real kicker — an increase of 9dB sounds twice as loud, but it takes double the power to change the level only 3dB!

Consequently, if we have a 100 watt system, we need to get close to 800 watts to sound twice as loud! (Crazy, ain't it?) But that's if it depended on amps alone, which it doesn't. As with wattage, doubling our speakers also yields a 3dB increase. In that case, getting up to 400 watts with twice as many speakers should add a total of about 9dB. We'll cover more about SPL and speaker efficiency in Chapter 10.

CHECKS & BALANCES

Amps take signals coming in and boost them tremendously, including any noise or *ground loops*[11]. So it's the same situation as the mixer input stage — *balanced*[10] inputs can become critical. Again, they eliminate noise picked up along the length of the cable and allow you to lift grounds that cause hum. Unless your equipment is situated close together and plugged into the same AC circuit, you shouldn't use an amp with unbalanced inputs. Otherwise, Murphy's Law dictates that you will most likely have problems. Wiring connections are the same as we discussed earlier.

Setting Level: As with mixers, the level controls on the amp should be set properly for the system. Optimum settings should drive the amp to maximum power when the mixer reaches the *nominal*[2] "0dB" reading on its meters. At some point just over 0dB, we should see an overload indication on the amp. This way, we will always know how hard our system is working by our meter readings.

An easy way to set amp levels without breaking up sinus congestion and glassware is to unhook the speakers from the amp. (Don't do this with a tube amp!) With strong music or pink noise from an analyzer running through the mixer, bring up the master level until the meter hits just above 0dB. (Of course, all subsequent processors like equalizers and crossovers should be set for unity gain so you don't lose level along the way.) Bring up the amp level until you see its **overload**, or **clipping**, indicator just start to illuminate. That's your setting. Now you may cut off the test source, hook up your speakers, and repeat after me: "I will not push my meters over the limit. I know that is all the power I have. I do not want to spend lots of money on repairs. Thank you Mr. White for saving my equipment. I'm sending $100 cash to show my appreciation."

If you find the system too loud for your needs with good meter readings, drop back the amp levels instead of the mixer. This will give you a better signal-to-noise ratio. Make note of the previous nominal amp settings for future reference in case you need to crank it up. If you can't quite get the amp to overload with the above procedure, you have my permission to raise graphic EQ or active crossover levels slightly to the point where it does. If it still won't, it's an indication you may have mismatched equipment. Ask a pro for help in pursuing the best solution.

Ohm, Sweet Ohm: Amplifier power is rated in relation to the amount of power 'draw' by the speakers. It's listed in the specifications of the amp and determined by the **impedance** of the speaker load. You will see amp wattages based on 8Ω (*ohm*), 4Ω, and sometimes 2Ω loads, and they should correspond at least to what your speakers can handle if you expect to drive them to full power. (More speakers are damaged by too little power than they are by too much due to the stress in trying to reproduce a distorted amp signal.) There's also a rating called **bridged mono** which we'll discuss shortly.

Most speakers are 8Ω and will indicate it near their connector plate. If you connect two 8Ω speakers to the same amp, the load halves and becomes 4Ω. You'll notice in amp specs that the wattage on a 4Ω load is typically one-third higher than 8Ω. So for the extra speaker we add, the amp provides more power. By the same token, two 4Ω loads make a 2Ω. However, the limit is usually 4Ω for most amps, below which they may eventually overheat and shut down. If our total speaker impedance load is too low, we will need more amps to accommodate them.

I will even go so far as to give you the only formula I intend to in this book:

$$Impedance \ = \ \frac{R1 \ x \ R2}{R1 \ + \ R2}$$

R1 equals the impedance of one speaker, and R2 equals that of a second.

For example, if we have an 8Ω and a 4Ω speaker: $\frac{8 \ x \ 4}{8 \ + \ 4} = \frac{32}{12} = 2.67Ω$

Obviously, this is too low for a minimum rating of 4Ω. So use this formula to make sure you're not overtaxing your amplifiers.

Amp Modes: Most professional amps are designed as a stereo, or dual, amplifier. They will operate as two amps in one package where each amp will handle its own load and can be used for individual purposes. Most have a special switch for different modes of operation. These include:

Stereo or Dual – each side of the amp receives its own source and functions independent of the other.

Parallel – the inputs of both amps are connected so they both receive a common source, though functioning independently in level settings and load.

Bridged Mono – both amps are electronically combined to form one BIG amp. *This is not meant as a designation for "non-stereo" applications!*

This mode is for rare occasions when you have a speaker requiring more power than one channel of an amp can provide. If I wish to drive one 400 watt speaker with a 200 watt per channel dual amp, I can switch it to Bridged Mono and turn it into a single 400 watt amp. (And now for my next trick. . .) Only the first channel of the amp provides input and level in this mode. Be advised, however, that most amps are only rated to 8Ω in bridged mode and there is a special method of hooking up the speakers as described on page 40. Please check your owner's manual for specifics.

70V Lines: In installations like churches or office buildings, you can end up with a mess of little speakers all over the place on ceilings, walls, under balconies, wherever! This obviously causes a problem with total impedance, so the audio geeks of yesteryear came up with another idea. A 70V connection is designated on amplifiers that have it, and must be used with speakers equipped with 70V transformers. They are designed exclusively for this application.

These speakers have separate wires tapped off their transformer for different wattages which we may choose for the speaker to draw. Since they are usually small 8" speakers, the taps are typically 0.5 to 10 watts. In this situation, we are concerned with total wattage consumption instead of impedance. With a 100 watt amp, we can run up to 20 speakers wired at 5 watts each: 20 x 5 = 100. Or 10 speakers at 10 watts each. Simple math. Just do it.

CONNECTORS & CABLES[9]

Inputs are generally the same RCA phono, 1/4" phone, or XLR connections as found on the mixer. Some common speaker output connections are phone plugs or **5-way binding posts**. These are dual screw-down posts allowing the connection of bare wire or **dual banana plugs**. For each side of a dual amp, there will be a red post for the **positive** (+) connector, and a black post for the **ground** (–). In Bridged Mono mode, the red post of the first side will be the *positive*, and the red post of the other side will be the *ground*. Always double check your manual for proper bridged connection.

Speaker connections themselves will include the same phone or banana plugs, or the more professional **Neutrik Speakon** connectors. These are durable four to eight conductor plugs designed to accommodate professional concert enclosures for single cable multi-component hookups.

Large gauge cable is used to carry the higher voltage output of amplifiers. Wires run side by side like AC cables and are not shielded like mic and line cables. There will be some conspicuous difference between the two wires for keeping positive and negative straight: copper/silver, white/black, ribbed/smooth, etc. Figuring for a 100 to 400 watt amp, I suggest a *minimum* of 16 gauge for cables up to 25', 14 gauge up to 50', and 12 gauge up to 100'. If in doubt, always go to the next larger gauge.

Going Through A Phase: I can't tell you how many times I have been to a performance or in a studio and heard speakers wired out of phase. Avoiding this just involves making sure the *positive* (+) connection of the speaker is hooked to the *positive* of the amp. *Double check yourself.* Otherwise, your sound will be screwy.

Your ears can also alert you with a quick test. With music playing, start in front of and facing one speaker, then gradually move towards the other speaker. When you get equidistant between the two, sound should appear centered. But if it suddenly sounds as if *everything* is split to both sides, they're out of phase. It's most likely the cable connections unless you had Goober rewire your cabinets.

If necessary, you can check to see if speaker cabinets are internally wired properly. With a cable plugged into the cabinet, quickly touch the positive and negative contacts of a 9V battery to the corresponding points on the other end of the cable. If the woofer jumps forward, everything's okay. If it jumps backward, connections are reversed. If it jumps sideways, seek counseling. If you can't see the woofer or don't know what it is, forget this test and proceed to Chapter 9.

Proper polarity is important not only for the center imaging, but to avoid loss of frequencies overall. Speakers out of phase are trying to cancel each other out. Once corrected, you'll notice better response from the whole system, and others will be amazed at your incredible ability to detect the problem. A good way to make new friends and an interesting topic at parties. Pass the chips.

10. PUMPING PAPER

If there is going to be a weak link in system design, it will most likely be the speakers. This is because they have the most going against them. As with microphones, we are in a delicate position of transforming between electrical and acoustical energy. But microphones are single small elements picking up within a relatively short distance, minimizing our room for error. Speakers, however, use multiple large components required to blend together and cover large distances. Consequently, how well things are designed becomes more critical.

S.P.L & R.U.Def

SPL[22] or *sound pressure level*, which we touched on in the Amp section as a reference to how we hear wattage changes, is a measurement of actual intensity levels which our speakers can generate. It is based on a 0dB threshold of hearing with normal conversation at about 70dB, a strong gospel church service around 100dB, and a rock concert capable of 120dB or more. Anything over 110dB can start getting uncomfortable depending on your tolerance, with 140dB considered the Official Threshold of Pain. Following are some of my examples of various levels (for best effect, please read from bottom up):

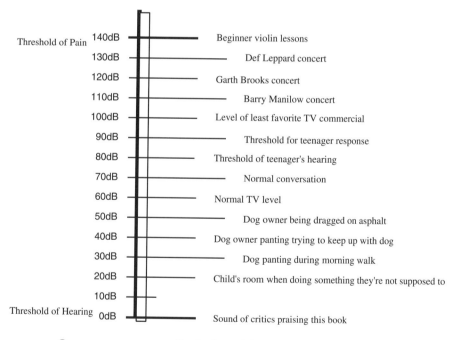

Threshold of Pain	140dB	Beginner violin lessons
	130dB	Def Leppard concert
	120dB	Garth Brooks concert
	110dB	Barry Manilow concert
	100dB	Level of least favorite TV commercial
	90dB	Threshold for teenager response
	80dB	Threshold of teenager's hearing
	70dB	Normal conversation
	60dB	Normal TV level
	50dB	Dog owner being dragged on asphalt
	40dB	Dog owner panting trying to keep up with dog
	30dB	Dog panting during morning walk
	20dB	Child's room when doing something they're not supposed to
	10dB	
Threshold of Hearing	0dB	Sound of critics praising this book

Our ears were actually designed for conversation. At speech levels, we have a peak in our hearing response around 3kHz where the definition is, while high and low end response is down considerably. In other words, we don't hear *flat*[21] at lower levels. This is the reason for a **loudness** switch on most hi-fi systems. It's a boost for the low and high end to compensate for our low level hearing response.

Yet an interesting thing happens when we start cranking up the volume. A little 'compressor' in our brain starts grabbing the 3kHz spot while the other frequencies rise to catch up, until the response finally flattens out at around 90dB. That's why music sounds better when it's louder — our ears are hearing it right! (Sorry, mom.)

For this reason, I'm usually going to be running music program to around 90dB in the studio when I want to hear things accurately. But I want to keep dynamic concert sound within the 120dB range to avoid hearing damage. The exception is low end which I can drive to slightly higher 'feel' levels, adding punch while avoiding excessive ear-damaging high frequency levels. Be aware, though, that long durations of any high levels can affect your hearing.

STACKING UP

Back in the old days (that's Woodstock to me), the norm was big and bunches. We had separate boxes for tweeters, horns, mids, midbass, bass, and Ripple. We had 4-way and 5-way crossovers. Hundreds of pounds of amps. And 'narly' sound, dude! That's because all these different components were doing their own thing and could rarely get it together. . . just like us.

With the vast improvements in speaker design and components, we now have systems that actually work together, take up less real estate, and sound good. We can get everything we need from **2-way** or **3-way speakers** and **subwoofers**, but how do we know which ones to get? Good hints are in the specifications of speakers, but they need to be looked at collectively. For instance, with near-field studio monitors, I'm mostly concerned with the **frequency response**. Larger PA speakers should also be considered for **sensitivity** and **polar response**.

Sensitivity: Now you can use all that stuff you learned about **SPL**[22] where "doublingwattageadds3dB" and "9dBistwicethevolume". Studio monitors, which are designed more for wide response and moderate levels, will have sensitivity listings around 87dB. PA speakers will be around 97dB, a 10dB increase. This means that if you hook up a PA speaker in place of a studio monitor (without changing the amp or level settings), it will sound at least twice as loud. Obviously, this is much better for high level applications. In fact, just a 3dB difference in speaker efficiency can mean an increase comparable to doubling wattage. Remember?

Frequency Response: So if we see one PA speaker listed at 97dB and another at 100dB, buy the second one, right? Wrong! First, you have to look at the frequency response graphs. They should appear as close to a *flat*[21] line as possible from 100Hz to over 15kHz. These may indicate that a louder speaker has a 4dB peak sticking up at 2kHz. So the speaker is louder due to a harsh peak which may also cause feedback. That isn't

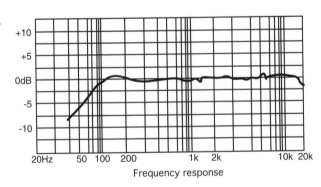

Frequency response

good. We don't want to sacrifice quality for volume. If that were the case, stadium horns would be perfect. (In fact, I believe that's what they use in Hell for the audiophile section.)

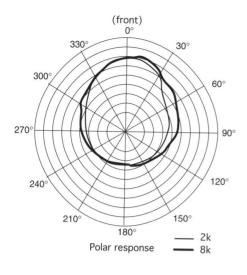

(front)
0°
330°   30°
300°   60°
270°   90°
240°   120°
210°   150°
180°
Polar response   —— 2k
                      —— 8k

Polar Response: PA speakers use horns to increase projection of high frequencies. Like a spotlight, horns *disperse*[23] these frequencies in a narrower pattern with higher velocity to throw farther in a large room. Unfortunately, the sound can get a little messed up from bouncing around in the horn chamber, so design is very critical.

A polar reponse graph tells us how good that design is. A great horn will show almost perfectly matched oval lines from 2kHz to 16kHz. A bad one will have all kinds of weird shapes. This represents frequencies that peak out at certain positions around the horn and drop out at others, changing your sound and level considerably throughout the room. *Where the frequency response curve tells how good the sound is directly in front of the cabinet, the polar response tells how good it is everywhere else!* All this taken into account, a good speaker design can become pretty obvious.

CROSSING OVER

You might remember I skipped over **crossovers** in the signal processing section. Well, now it's time! These units help speakers do their job better and with less potential for damage. That's because they allow the various components to receive only the frequencies they're best designed for.

Full range speakers have 2 or 3 components: a **woofer** for low frequencies, a **tweeter** for high frequencies, and sometimes an additional **midrange** driver dedicated to frequencies between the other two. Since the tweeter is very small compared to the woofer, it can't move enough to reproduce the lower frequencies and will be damaged by them. So the crossover filters out the low end going to the tweeter. Alternately, the woofer won't be damaged by high frequencies but does a sloppy job of reproducing the ones it can. So the crossover filters the highs from the low frequency components. Similar concessions are made for a midrange driver, with its range usually somewhere between 500Hz and 5kHz.

Most full range speakers have a **passive crossover** (non-powered) built-in. This network takes the speaker signal coming in from the amplifier and does the filtering before it goes to the components in the cabinet. An **active crossover** is an external powered unit which receives the line level signal from the mixer, then splits the frequencies *before the amps*. The individual amplifiers then provide their specific ranges directly to the appropriate components. Advantages to these powered units are that crossover points are more precise and may be adjusted, independent levels can be set for the various frequency ranges, and each amplifier can work a little easier doing a specific job.

Except in high-power concert applications, the quality of current internal passive crossovers is adequate for typical full range purposes. It's when using subwoofers that the active crossover becomes an essential addition as we'll learn in a moment.

STUDIO MONITORS

In the recording studio, we need an accurate set of speakers since every move we make is based on what we hear. Unlike many hi-fi speakers which are designed more for subjective and cosmetic appeal, studio monitors are designed with *flat response*[21] as a priority. The term implies smooth and accurate, not 'bland' like a carbonated drink gone bad. With an accurate reference, we will be able to mix recordings well suited to all types of speakers.

Studio monitors are usually 2-way designs with woofers from 6" to 8", or 3-way with woofers of 10" to 15". They'll typically use 1" dome tweeters and 3-5" midrange drivers, though some larger models employ horns. Some popular manufacturers include JBL, KRK, and Yamaha. Tannoy and Urei have offered models using coaxial speakers which employ a tweeter horn mounted in the middle of the woofer.

Active monitors have a built-in amp and active crossover to maximize the capabilities of the system. Though understandably higher in cost, they exhibit exceptional efficiency and sound quality. Two high-end brands are Meyer and Genelec. Well worth the price if it's in your budget.

When choosing monitors, as with any speaker, the specs can tell us much of what we want to know but listening will tell us the most. All good speakers sound a little different and our preferences are subjective, so pick one that appeals to you. And if you're not used to an accurate speaker, a good one will teach you a lot about how things *should* sound.

PA SPEAKERS

Full range speakers use 10" to 15" woofers and horn drivers of 1" to 2", and most are 2-way since current high end drivers do such a good job through the upper ranges. Some cabinets use cheaper **piezo** horns which should be avoided in critical applications. These elements are 'beamy' and only reproduce above 6kHz, skipping right over the critical 2-5kHz presence range. True **compression driver** horns offer wide dispersion and response as well as better power handling.

I like staying with single woofer designs, and consider it errant to buy large dual-woofer full range with the idea that they will give you best overall performance. It is much more efficient and similarly cost-effective to keep the full range compact and elevated for projection, and add **subwoofers** when you require powerful low end. It also makes 10" to 12" full range more feasible since they're not required to handle bass, improving mid definition for vocals along with size, weight, and cost considerations. (By the way, this is called the **satellite** approach where smaller elevated speakers are used in conjunction with floor-level subs.)

Waveguides: One of the more exciting developments in PA horn design is the circular waveguide which has been offered by Yamaha, WorxAudio, Bag End, and a few others. Since high frequencies emanate in a spherical pattern from a *round* driver, it makes sense to have a circular horn to best retain their natural characteristics and avoid the transformation problems of changing a circle to a square. In my opinion, it's the closest I've heard to true high-fidelity in affordable PA speakers, and I personally believe most designs should be using circular waveguide horns.

Subwoofers: Subwoofers are usually single or dual 15" or 18" enclosures. I normally prefer dual 15" for their efficiency and naturally 'tight' sound. Subs should be dedicated to their own frequency range below 80Hz to 125Hz, and are specifically designed to maximize low end potential. An active crossover will provide this range to the sub and filter low frequencies out of our full range so they can work cleaner and easier. The full range can be elevated for coverage and the subwoofer(s) kept on the floor for maximum efficiency.

The reason for this is the omnidirectionality of low end. It uses planes, like a floor or wall, as an acoustic 'amplifier' to increase level in the room. In fact, I can get at least 6dB more bass and more even distribution throughout most rooms by placing the sub on the floor and pointing it towards a wall, within a few inches or a few feet. I've done churches with 3 or 4 small hanging speakers, and a single sub placed to the back and side of the stage area this way. Unless you're standing beside it, you don't know where the low end is coming from! People just assume the full range speakers sound that incredible.

Spot Check: Particular attention should be given to the horn *dispersion*[23] in PA systems. Just as with mic pickup, we can direct speakers like spotlights to cover the necessary areas. Plus, we want our stage mics to be out of the horn pattern to minimize feedback. Floor monitors (compact wedge versions of our full range) are designed to cover your stage needs.

Put your wrists together and angle your palms out to form a right angle. Then point out toward the room, and you can approximate the area a typical 90° horn should cover. Systems with 60-75° horns can throw more evenly over a longer distance, so I prefer these if I have to carry more than 50 feet. Just narrow the palm angle slightly to spot check.

Another concern is if you have to hit a balcony. You can adjust the 'palm' thing sideways to get some idea if a typical 45° vertical pattern will catch it. Waveguide horns make this easier since their pattern is 60-75° all around. If the pattern isn't high enough, additional speakers or horns will be needed for balcony coverage.

Stage Monitors: Monitor enclosures will essentially be slant versions of our 2-way full range using 10" to 15" woofers. There are also smaller designs like the Galaxy Hot Spot with only one or two 5" to 6" speakers. They're especially useful for providing good mid/high definition to one or two performers within a small area, and minimizing excessive low end bleed into the room caused by larger, 'bassier' floor monitors.

A relatively recent development is the **wireless in-ear monitor (IEM)** now used in many major concert tours. These high-grade devices use an audio transmitter and individual receiver packs that operate in stereo on UHF frequencies, utilize special earpieces that block outside sound, and have dropped to under $1000 from companies like Shure and Sennheiser. The Sennheiser Evolution system has a cost-saving "dual-mono" mode which allows two monitor feeds from a single transmitter to be individually selectable on multiple receiver packs.

Where cost is a deterrent, there are wireless hearing-assistance systems by Telex and Phonic Ear that I have used with some decent results in this application though they don't offer the quality of the UHF systems and can be noisy if reception is weak or good levels aren't fed to the transmitter. In any case, wireless in-ear can eliminate the amplifiers, cabling, stage monitor levels, and potential feedback of monitor speakers while offering a perfect mix that follows your artist to the ends of the earth (if you can transmit that far).

Companies like HearTechnologies and Aviom offer affordable multichannel, wired in-ear systems with significant advantages when freedom of movement is minimal. These handle a combination of 8 to 16 feeds from auxes, insert sends, direct outs, etc. to a multichannel hub. The hub then sends all signals through a cable to individual remotes with separate level controls for each feed. Everyone controls their own personal monitor mix, and cost can be as low as $200 per person. Hook the earphone output of the remote to a wireless IEM transmitter, and you'll have both mix control and untethered movement. (With any IEM, be aware of the possibility of hearing damage if users aren't smart about adjusting their earphone levels, and hygiene concerns if earpieces are used by different people.)

DELAY LINES[18]

If you have seating out of the throw or line-of-sight of the main speakers, such as under a balcony, you will need speakers dedicated to the area. Whether extra full range or small ceiling speakers, they will need to be on a high quality delay unit placed before their amplifier to compensate for distances of 40' or more between them and the main speakers. Otherwise, you will have a noticeable echo between the two.

The delay time should be set at just under 1 millisecond per foot of distance between the main and delayed speakers, or you may tune it by ear with a well-defined rhythm source such as drums on a pre-recorded tape. While listening in the delayed area, have someone at the delay unit increase the delay time setting until you hear the echo disappear between the main and delayed speakers, and the rhythm hits occur simultaneously. From that point, increase the delay time another 5ms and the delayed speakers will almost seem to disappear. This is a result of the *Haas effect*[19], as mentioned in the Delay section. When the room

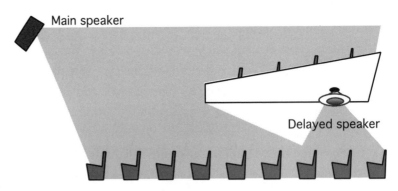

Main speaker

Delayed speaker

delay is set just a few milliseconds longer than needed, the ear is fooled into thinking the sound is coming from the original source. It's important, however, that the delayed system level and EQ be set to only supplement the mains as needed. Most of the time, subtle mid/high definition is all that's required. Low and low-mid frequencies from the main speakers will usually reach or reflect into the delayed areas, adding body and supporting the **point-source reference** (sound perceived to emanate from the direction of the source).

11. FOR THE RECORD

RECORDING

Well, hasn't recording technology just blown wide open in the last decade! With the advent of Modular Digital Multitracks (MDMs) and hard disk systems at the end of the 20th century, world-class multitrack was available to the masses. Economical semi-pro tape recorders had served us well, but they were rendered obsolete by the quality, convenience, and expandability of these new systems. Technically, digital had its own set of problems to overcome, but current products truly offer a level of performance previously unimagined in their price range. What gives digital recording this potential for inherent superiority? Let me offer a simple illustration:

An architect in Virginia prepares artwork of a house for a fellow architect in California. Once finished, he makes a copy of his final draft and faxes it out to his associate. As you can imagine, a good bit of quality and detail will be lost in the transition by attempting to pass the original through this entire 'analog' process.

On the other hand, let's say the same architect opts to print a list of specific instructions describing dimensions, angles, features, Pantone colors, etc. of the drawing. He makes a copy and sends a fax. Even if only barely readable, his associate can redraw a perfect version from the instructions. This is the 'digital' process.

In recording, the sound is turned into digital instructions (1's and 0's) by an **analog-to-digital converter** and printed to tape. When played back, the digital info is 'redrawn' to analog form by a **digital-to-analog converter**. Result: a beautiful picture!

Digital Domains: The thing that never ceases to amaze me is that the sounds we hear can be represented by a single waveform (two for stereo). And from that waveform, which a speaker is reproducing with sound pressure changes as it moves back and forth, our magical ears can distinguish anything from a solo acoustic guitar to the collective instruments of a 60-piece orchestra. It is this complex waveform that the recording process must capture accurately.

In the digital domain, we can see this waveform drawing as a graph. The vertical graduations are represented by the **bit resolution**. 16-bit means we have 16 numbers and two possibilities for each number, a 1 or a 0. The total number of possibilities are 2^{16} or 65,536. The horizontal graduations are represented by the **sampling rate**, usually 48,000 times per second. So for each 1/48,000th of a second, we can put a dot on one of over 65,000 vertical points to plot our waveform— pretty fine detail if you ask me. And if we go to 20-bit technology, we'll have over 1,000,000 vertical points to choose from! This means an even smoother drawing with more dynamic range (the amount of headroom we have available for level from our softest to loudest passages). All in all, the higher the resolution, the clearer and more accurate the reproduction. At this printing, we've seen recording get to 24-bit/96k-sampling and processing to 56-bit!

Why am I telling you all this? So you'll have a little better understanding of the technology that's permeating every aspect of audio — recorders, effects, signal processors *and* mixers. Who would have thought a few years ago that today you could have a complete digital multitrack and mixing system for under $5000? (Nostradamos said nothing about it.)

RECORDERS

Professional 24-track analog recorders using 2" reel tape are still a studio standard. Like tube technology, analog has unique musical characteristics based on the subtle ways it changes sound rather than its total perfection in reproducing it. But $25,000+ for a quality machine plus 2" tape costs at 30 IPS (inches per second) can put a serious crunch on the average musician's budget.

The new digital recorders and **workstations** (recorder/mixer combinations) offer high-quality reproduction at much lower cost, and unprecedented capabilities only possible with digital technology. Though there's been a lot of argument over analog vs. digital, there is no question where the market is heading. Personally I welcome all that digital has to offer, and have found ways to duplicate desired analog characteristics as needed using creative micing, EQ, compression, and/or tube processing.

Digital Tape Recorders: These MDMs use high-resolution **SVHS** or **Hi8** video tape to record digital audio. Adapting a digital format to economical and readily available video transports brought costs down to those previously associated with semi-pro tape machines. The advantages over these were numerous:

1. There is no inherent tape noise to contend with.
2. There's no need for sound degrading noise reduction.
3. Spot editing (punch in/punch out) is totally seamless.
4. You can bounce or transfer tracks with no loss of quality.
5. Audio reproduction is consistent from machine to machine.
6. Synchronizing of multiple machines is simple and much more accurate.
7. Complex software-based functions are possible such as digital routing, track delay, and programmed recording.

They function pretty much like a normal tape recorder, just with all the added capabilities. The only maintenance is periodic cleaning which is the same as for a video deck. Head life is estimated at 2000 hours or more. At least one brand will even tell you how many actual hours of use are on the head.

A unique feature is their inherent ability to synchronize together for more tracks. Big reel machines require expensive servo motors and synchronizers to lock together. The MDMs need only loosely sync the motors; digital buffers make sure the audio is output precisely to timecode clocked at 48,000 times a second! It's also much more cost-effective to manufacture a single 8-track model rather than divide production between 16 and 24-track models, too. Now you can just buy as many 8-tracks as you need and lock them up. They can be synced to video or MIDI sequencing gear as well, and clocked with interfaces to the internal timecode which is already part of the digital information.

Digital multitracks can be set to 48k or 44.1k sampling rate, the latter being the CD manufacturing standard. Recording time per tape varies from 40 to 100 minutes depending on the machine you use. The ADAT system has the capability of unlimited pre-programmed 'overlapped' recording and playback time using its master remote control with multiple machines paralleled. It also allows you to store complex system setups and numerous locate points on the tape for future recall, a convenient and time-saving feature in commercial or educational recording facilities.

Hard Disk Recorders: These units offer all the advantages of digital recording plus random access location and editing capabilities. Like CDs, you can go to any point on your recording instantaneously as well as copy, delete, and move things around. This is possible since information is being read off a computer hard disk as opposed to a linear piece of tape.

Many systems are totally software-based and require a compatible computer, but there are a few self-contained systems. Most offer **waveform editing** as an integral or optional feature. This allows you to actually display the waveform on a screen where you can do creative (or wacky) things to it: edit out noises or breath sounds, alter whole words, duplicate parts, etc. Loads of fun for the whole family!

You can also create different versions of a recording. Re-recording various sections to other locations is the copy method. Another feature called the **playlist**, however, allows you to designate different sections of a recording and simply program them to be played back in different arrangements without copying and using up more disk memory.

Hard disk recorders have become very economical and are driving the older digital tape units to extinction, though available memory is at the mercy of present (but rapidly progressing) technology. Internal hard disk size can range from 540 megabytes, which holds about 100 minutes of 16-bit audio, to 20 gigabytes (20,000 megabytes) or more for over 60 hours worth! This is total time which you'll have to divide by the number of recorded tracks and reduce for higher resolution recording. In other words, 100 minutes total time is only 12.5 minutes per track for 8-track, 16-bit recording. Hookups for external SCSI drives can offer even more memory for recording and archiving, and CDR storage can be convenient for up to 700MB of data on a removable medium in addition to being an audio mastering format. There are also emerging "data compression" schemes and newer formats like DVD-Pro that stand ready to increase recording time and capabilities.

MiniDisc (or MD) Recorders: The Sony MiniDisc format was exploited in the multitrack market for a time with 4-track and 8-track units by Sony, Yamaha, and Tascam. The MDs offer most of the advantages of hard disk but on a cost-effective and removable MD Data Disc which holds about 140 minutes total time, eliminating the need for offloading data. They also proved useful for live production stereo soundtracks in theatre with instant cueing like CDs, song titling, and extra tracks for adding voiceovers, sound effects, and overlapping song transitions. MDs utilize a proprietary data compression scheme, so they were never deemed a 'full-quality' professional format.

Magneto-Optical (MO) Recorders: MO was a promising format that got lost in the transitional shuffle of new technologies, falling somewhere between a recordable CD and a MiniDisc: random access, re-recordable, housed in a casing (like MD), available in 3.5" and 5" versions, and recording non-compressed audio. Though first introduced by Akai with their earlier DD1000 2-track, it surfaced again in short-lived modular 8-track models by HHB and Yamaha. Everything you always wanted in a MiniDisc... and more.

DAT Recorders: Digital **A**udio **T**ape recorders were the first affordable digital format available. Originally designed as a consumer product, it was soon clear that consumers wouldn't take the bait and DATs ended up being adopted by the pro audio industry as the standard format for cassette and CD manufacture. They record stereo digital audio on special DAT tapes sharing a single data track, and are not capable of punch in/out editing or recording separate tracks. Though subject to the normal wear of tape and mechanics, they established their reliability over the years. There were even a few portable 'Walkman-type' models which I loved to sneak into concerts or Presidential cabinet meetings.

DATs will record up to 120 minutes of audio at 48kHz or 44.1kHz standards, and some have the capability of 32kHz "non-linear" long play recording for up to four hours. This limits frequency response to about 15kHz, so I only use it for non-critical programs, lectures, and saving my old record albums, scratches and all.

CD Recorders (CDR): I'm sure you're acquainted with CDs, but it's really only in recent years that we've had affordable, recordable, portable, wish-we'd-had-'em-before-dable CD recorders. Two versions have been available: pro CDR which records on standard blank CDs, and CDRW which is a consumer format that records on special version CDs. The reason for the latter was to give record companies a little protection from mass-population pirating. CDRW recorders are cheaper and the special CDs can be re-recorded on (unlike write-once pro CDs), but each CD costs more than the pro format because a "duplication dividend" is collected for the record companies with each sale. They also incorporate "copy prohibit" in the format to prevent direct digital copies from being made.

When we finally had the luxury of mix automation with the digital mixers, I switched to CD for my mastering medium. Before affordable automation, we were destined to make numerous attempts at the final mix, trying to get all those knob and fader moves just right. Since write-once pro CDs could not be re-recorded after a mistake, re-recordable DAT was our logical choice. But now automation can be our master! All our settings and moves are recorded in the mix software so you just start the CDR, hit the 'automix' button, and a perfect mix is transferred while you sit back and enjoy your prune juice. Ain't technology great? The Yamaha AW4416 16-track workstation (as a current example) has mix automation, an extra stereo track for mixdown, and a built-in CDR for mastering and data storage.

It won't be long for this section to make the Smithsonian with all the current advances in digital audio. Eventually, all digital equipment should be able to fully integrate and communicate. The near future should spawn more in recordable/removable multitrack disc, googlabytes of random-access memory (RAM), and maybe even Dilithium-crystal recording with Warp drives! Stardate... sooner than you think.

Cassette Multitracks: For the beginners or cost-conscious, there may still be a few 4-track cassette recorders on the store shelves. They use standard high bias cassettes, and have a basic mixer with adequate quality and EQ control. They're easy to use and provide a useful experience in recording and production techniques.

Regular stereo cassette players are 4-track formats, but they only record stereo tracks (left and right) on one edge of the tape. When you flip the tape over, it records stereo tracks on the other edge in the opposite direction. Cassette multitracks record all 4 tracks simultaneously or individually in the same direction covering the whole tape, so you don't flip the tape over. For better quality, most units run at twice the speed of normal stereo decks. Think of it as more tape going by providing more 'memory' space for storing high frequency information.

When complete, your multitrack recording can be mixed to a regular stereo recording deck. Of course, you can't play a 4-track cassette recording on a regular cassette player for several reasons: it only plays two of the tracks at once, the other two are going in the wrong direction, high speed recording will result in very slow playback, and noise reduction may not be compatible (like DBX or Dolby S). But who am I to say. . . you may like your music this way!

A common procedure in multitracking and with 4-tracks specifically is **bouncing** or **ping-ponging**. This involves recording three tracks, then mixing and re-recording them together to track 4. Once finished, you can erase those first three tracks and record three new things on them. Or record two and bounce those to track 3. You can end up with 7 or more total tracks, but you lose considerable quality along the way. (Remember, this is analog.) When you're ready for better quality, you simply spend a little more and go digital.

VIRTUAL TRACKING

If you have keyboards, sound modules, and/or drum machines and MIDI sequencing capability, you already have a 'digital recording' system. Though it only plays back MIDI parts, you can synchronize it to a digital multitrack and have both play together in perfect time. This is called **MIDI sync**, and we even used to do it with tape multitracks using a tape-to-sync interface like the J.L. Cooper PPS-2. With most digital systems, MIDI sync can work in both directions (either sequencer as master and multitrack as slave or vice versa), and it will tell the slave when and where to start and how fast to go.

Suddenly, all your sequenced outputs become additional live tracks playing along with your multitrack system. You won't need to record these parts and use up tracks, you can make quick changes at any time by simply editing your sequences, and any keyboards or modules you add become more MIDI tracks. All you need is additional mixer channels to handle the extra outputs which, it so happens, are available or expandable on some digital workstations.

12. AUDIO BY DESIGN

It's time I confessed something, and it will probably blow any semblance of credibility and wisdom I've attempted to build to this point. . . "I bought a used 1987 Hyundai." There, I said it, but let me explain. I got a good deal. (Obviously.) It looked to be in good shape. (Okay, I wasn't wearing my glasses.) Everything seemed to be put together well. (So now I'm an accomplished automotive engineer!) And the thing was an endless deluge of disenchantment.

Somehow I missed the point. In considering its apparent outward condition, I overlooked a more important concept. . . something having to do with *MOTION*. The same thing can happen with audio. You need some idea of what you're trying to achieve, or you're going nowhere. All the fancy tools are worthless without a master plan. I hope to start you on a basic blueprint in this section.

RECORDING

The studio is the most controlled and critical audio environment, making it a great spot to sharpen your skills, train your ears, and experiment with ideas. Unlike live sound situations, there are few background noises and room resonances to mask the audio details you need to hear, you have the luxury of being able to do "one more take" until you get it the way you want it, and you have an excellent reference on which to base your results — national quality recordings. You can even listen to them side by side with your projects to make immediate comparisons and corrections.

You need some idea of what you're trying to achieve, or you're going nowhere.

If things sound too good to be true, they are. There is an inherent problem with recording that the uninitiated fail to consider. In a live performance, you have sound arriving at your ears from a multitude of sources and directions. Each ear receives these as soundwaves with all kinds of complex location information to help separate and clarify the different components and direction of the sounds.

In stereo production, all this needs to be duplicated by only two speakers, two positions. A lot of critical information is missing, limiting the ear's ability to distinguish the sources and their placement clearly. So we must compensate somehow to help simulate (and stimulate) the 'transparency' of the natural environment. This is done with what I call **"The Five P's of Production."**

Frequency Pockets[7]: Vocals, guitars, keyboards, bass, horns, drums. . . all this conglomeration gets jammed through speakers and suddenly it's like a small room crowded with people. They're stepping on each others toes, and it's hard to see who's who. If we can dress them all in different colored clothes and spread them out more, maybe we can improve the situation.

In mixing, the different instruments can quickly start muddling together, especially in the lower frequencies where bass starts piling up. *My first fix is to roll bass EQ out of non-bass sources.* Voices, guitars, horns, most keyboard parts, etc. don't have much if any low end below 100Hz. What *is* there usually consists of boominess or muddiness that will get in the way of bass and bass drum, and destroy clarifying contrast between low and high end sounds. So take it out on appropriate channels to the point where the sound clears up, but before it gets overly thin.

Next, we'll start identifying and dedicating the frequency ranges where our individual instruments best fit. For example, bass drum 'feel' is concentrated around 60-70Hz, so maybe I'll EQ the bass guitar for the 70-200Hz range with definition up to 1kHz. Keyboards may provide warmth and body through the 200-600Hz range with some nice highs up to 6kHz, so I'll EQ the lead guitar to stand out in the 500-800Hz range with good bite at 2kHz. I might also take frequencies above 8kHz out of both to make room for the high end 'brilliance' of vocals and cymbals. Sax will fit nicely in the 700Hz-5kHz spot and vocals, with their slightly higher levels, should predominate from 400Hz to 12kHz. Cymbals will top everything off with sweet highs added up over 12kHz.

Though these are only examples and other frequencies are present in all these instruments, giving each its own special 'pocket' makes them more discernable and evens out levels throughout the frequency spectrum. In fact, with a realtime analyzer hooked up, you can get visual indication where each instrument is in the mix, and experiment with getting a smoother response on your recordings. As I discussed in the section on equalizers, much of this is accomplished by cutting back non-essential frequencies rather than heavily boosting the desired ones. This takes a bit of work, and lends itself to the next important aspect of mixing.

Priorities (Also known as Commitment): No room for 'wishy-washy' Charlie Browns here. When I use creative EQ to improve overall balance and separation, I also commit to something definite which listeners will be able to identify and relate to. And I can choose to be conspicuously different or even radical in this endeavor, attracting attention to the music and its components.

Such easily recognizable aspects of a song, in composition *or* production, are called **hooks**. The more good ones you have, the more likely the song will be noticed. The same concept applies to instrument balance. Everybody can't be the 'star'. *Pick the strongest and most dominant themes and commit those out front.* Mix the rest comfortably in the background to create a good foundation of support. If there isn't a dominant memorable theme, create one! Don't just jam up a bunch of weak ideas. The song is only as strong as its weakest link.

Sometimes it may seem hard to keep priorities like vocals from getting enveloped by other sounds. The trick is using pockets along with keeping the denser instruments lower in the mix. You may need to EQ down the 2-4kHz range on keyboards or distortion guitar to make more room for vocal presence. I prefer to get more power out of my mixes by kicking the drums strong since they offer a lot of open spaces for the vocals to come through. Then my rhythm instruments will altogether equal the level of the drums. Bass is adjusted to add fullness to the overall mix. Finally, I'll ride the leads and instrumental hooks, bringing them up and down to fill in gaps between vocal parts.

Be aware of the tendency for vocals to collectively exceed a desired overall level. When harmony parts come in, don't bring them up to the lead. Rather, have them set at least 3dB lower and blend the lead back into them, maintaining a more consistent overall level and avoiding peaks.

Panning[15]: We'll use the stereo channel pans to move things left and right in the mix and create a 2-dimensional image. I designate settings as clock positions: 9:00, 2:00, 12:00, etc. Except for actual stereo tracks such as keyboards, effects, or stereo mic pairs, I usually don't pan sources full left and right. It can sound like one ear is stopped up if I'm wearing headphones.

I also give a lot of consideration to panning sources with similar characteristics to opposite sides for better balance and separation. If the hi hat is panned right, the high end percussive acoustic guitar is left. If sax is left, lead guitar is right. Sopranos right, altos left and so on. Pan everything a little differently to maximize separation, and make sure your left/right metering maintains an even balance.

Perspective: Mic technique can be a critical aspect in creating a 3-dimensional perspective. *Stereo micing*[5] is one of the most effective because it captures natural room characteristics recognizable to our ears. The better the room, the better the effect. And using this technique for recording background vocalists or other multiple sources all together provides the imaging of each element being in a unique position in the mix.

When close-micing a single source, you can place another mic back in the room to pick up the ambience. Pan the two to opposite sides in the mix and you get another nice natural effect.

Try switching *phase reverse*[14] on some channels if you have it available. This is a feature on high end consoles and is used to switch the polarity of the source signal. I've used it on background vocals, cymbals, and high end percussion with some slight but noticeable changes in front-to-back perspective.

Of course, there are a few black boxes offering 3-D and surround alternatives, but we must assume that many won't be compatible on other systems. Used discreetly, some like the earlier Hughes Retriever gave me successful results on specific stereo tracks such as drum overheads, background vocals, and stereo effects, pulling them out in front of the speaker plane as much as a foot. If you get a chance, experiment with the potential of these new devices. You may come up with your own sound and special effects.

Processing: Digital effects are the second stage of developing our 3-dimensional image, with *reverbs*[20] being the most useful addition. These will simulate the space of a variety of rooms. An easy way to make a source sound more distant is to roll off EQ above 5kHz and add more reverb, simulating the added ambience and loss of high end over distance. Another technique I use is recording a lead vocal twice, then mixing the first dry and the second as *full* reverb (no original signal) subtly blended in. The slight timing differences between the two make for a deeper, more dimensional sound. You may also set reverb **pre-delay** for an intended room depth, i.e. 80ms for 80 feet.

Along with some additional notes in the Effects section, there are endless possibilities that you'll just have to jump in and explore.

LIVE RECORDING

I've had a few people recently who wanted to have the capability of multitrack recording and live mixing simultaneously. The problem with using direct and group outs from the live console to the multitrack is that any EQ or level adjustments for the house mix are going to be printed to tape, and they may not be conducive to good tracks. A better approach might be to invest in some 8-channel rackmount mic preamps, three of which can feed 24 tracks. Just send mic lines through these to the multitrack, set levels with enough headroom at the soundcheck, and let it roll. Either a split snake or the multitrack outputs (in Input mode) can be fed to the live console, and a totally independent mix for the house can be achieved. Another option is using channel inserts as pre-fader sends (discussed on page 31) if distance is short since lines will be unbalanced. Inserts should be pre-EQ as well so that EQ changes on the house mix will not affect recording.

As I briefly mentioned in the Microphone section, orchestral recording can be accomplished with just a quality ***stereo pair***[5] in the hall. With multitrack capability, however, we have the luxury of section micing to give us more mix control. One concern of mine is the potential distance and delay between the hall mics and any section mics used. Solutions are minimizing the distance or using new high-resolution digital ***delay***[18]. In the studio, we can delay those section tracks to match the hall mics, achieving a perfect combination of natural stereo sound along with intimate instrumental detail and balance. In other words, you can have your cake and eat it too!

If you're just doing a stereo feed off the board, you may find your record mix balance a little off. The live mix is a calculated blend of system *and* ambient sound with the softer elements like vocals or violins reinforced more, the louder elements like brass or percussion reinforced less. By contrast, the tape *only* sees the system signal which may result in soft stuff blasting and loud stuff in the background. The smaller the room, the more pronounced the inconsistency. It's best to use dual or stereo post-fader aux outputs, or a split-feed to another mixer so compensated level adjustments can be made to the individual channels, creating a custom balance of your mix for stereo recording.

Final Notes: Here are some last minute tips before you fall into the piteous pit of perpetual production pursuits:

- Always get good levels to tracks, even with digital. It improves digital resolution and will aid console signal-to-noise.
- Don't overdue low end! If you want to hear a 9dB boost below 60Hz, hook up subwoofers. Don't try to cram it on tracks and eat up your dynamic range.
- Use compressors conservatively for the least side effects. If you wish to mildly limit the whole stereo mix, invest in a good tube model for best results.
- When recording a drum set, get at least one minute of just toms and cymbals at the head of the track(s). This will make it easier to get mixdown settings on them since they are usually sparse in the music itself.
- If lacking in effects units, print the less ambient ones to tape like echoes, pitch shift, etc. Save dimensional reverbs and delays for the final mix.
- Always check your final mixes at low volume levels where your ears become a 'mid-reference'. Listen for overall balance, making sure the instruments don't get wimpy in relation to the vocals. Everything should still be distinct.
- Always commend any producer on how lovely (he/she) looks today.

CLUB & CONCERT SOUND

I chose to cover recording first, because most of the critical aspects will carry over beautifully here. Obviously, studio quality sound would be optimum, but it is difficult to achieve due to the nature of this 'uncontrolled' environment. (This implies that you will be forced to adapt to the characteristics of the many venues you may be performing in.) Fortunately, the energy and visual stimulation of a live performance help mask many of the flaws and add to the overall impact of the sound, but we'll still have to deal with room acoustics, stage volume, background noise, speaker tuning, level and coverage requirements, and hecklers demanding Lynyrd Skynyrd and Mötley Crüe. And that's just in a Christian concert!

High wattage and levels are major concerns here. The whole idea of a concert is to be conspicuous, dynamic, and spectacular, and this must be maintained over any competing levels from enthusiastic crowd response. Unfortunately, most groups are trying to squeeze too much out of an inadequate system. If you have quality speakers well matched to amplification, system gain set up properly, mixer meters hitting at *nominal*[2] "0" and you still don't have enough level, you need more speakers and amps. Simple. *Save up!*

In live sound, I find myself pushing the 60Hz low end of the system a little hotter to increase 'punch' and perceived level without resorting to excessive high frequencies. Depending on the room, I may also add a touch more above 10kHz to carry brilliance. I'll make up headroom with **subsonic filtering**, taking out frequencies below 40Hz on my master EQ. This tightens up the bottom end and saves wattage.

When you're hooking up your system, also be aware of the current draw of all your amplifiers. It is usually listed on the back of the amps by the AC cord or fuse, and is listed in amperes such as "8A." If they only show *AC* wattage (not the speaker wattage), use the formula

WATTAGE ÷ 110 = AMPERES. (The 110 is the voltage off the wall.) The reason you need to know this is so you don't overload the AC wall circuits, most of which are only 20A each, or power strips which are only 15A each. Use 30-40A circuits if available, and divide up the amps to different circuits if necessary. Be aware of the potential for ground loops if you do.

The *Few Less* P's of *Performance* Production: Why less? Because we aren't concerned with *perspective* since the live room creates that. Even *processing* is applied more as special effect, since rooms will define their own ambience. The other three P's take on some unique perspectives.

Frequency pockets can be an advantage here, too. They help in the studio due to the limitations of speaker reproduction. In the live venue, it's due to the cluttering nature of room acoustics. You will also find your equalizing based on the combination of live and electronic sound. If the sound of the stage amps or monitors produce a lot of low and low mid in the room, you will be more conservative in this area through the main system.

Priorities need to be maintained, and are often in competition with stage levels. Use creative ideas to limit these levels in smaller venues. When instrument amps are mic'ed, coax the performers to face them across stage or back at themselves like stage monitors, and run their volumes at the lowest acceptable levels. Use plexiglass baffles around drums when necessary. (Unfortunately, this does nothing for offensive drum*mers*.) Use your ear, or analyzer, to determine which lower frequencies from the stage monitors are most pronounced in the room and drop these another 3-6dB on the monitor graphic. Many times I choose to EQ everything below 100Hz out of the monitors. This reduces excessive bass buildup on stage and in the room, and gives the monitor system more headroom. All this can greatly improve your control of the mix out front.

Panning[15] brings up another aspect of live sound — whether you should run a monaural or stereo system. Mono is fine, but these days it's usually just as economical to run stereo with several advantages. First, most stereo sources such as keyboards or stereo effects have a richer, cleaner sound when their imaging is maintained. Second, sources panned out slightly from each other can take on a little more separation and distinction. Third, the house signal is divided between two output busses (Left & Right) as opposed to one, increasing overall headroom through the system.

A valid concern has been that people sitting close to main speakers on one side would miss sources that are panned toward the other. But I've found that slight panning within 10:00 and 2:00 is subtle enough to be indiscernible level-wise, and the full-panned stereo sources *do* come out both sides with slight imaging differences that normally aren't a problem. The drum set also gets a nice effect from position panning in larger rooms. When run properly, I favor the idea that the majority of the audience is getting all the stereo advantages.

Many systems are forced to run mono when the operator prefers *grouping*[16] all his channels. On 4 or 8 group consoles, the pans are used in conjunction with the assign switches to feed multiple channels out a common group fader for *submaster* control. Then the groups are fed to the main outs. The problem is that all the channels sent to a group are routed through a single fader, hence they all become mono. For something like stereo drums, you would have to assign to two groups panned in stereo which uses up available groups twice as fast.

Another way around this is to route all your critical stereo stuff directly to the main stereo outs. All the other stuff can be grouped as desired. Interestingly enough, the new digital mixers offer the best of both worlds. Since their fader groups are created by linking the individual motorized faders of the channels, no mono routing is necessary. Each channel is free to pan, allowing you to group *and* maintain full stereo flexibility!

Cluster: While you local 'road' engineers may be envisioning side stacks of speakers, a ***central cluster***[24] is the popular arrangement in fixed installations. Though it doesn't have the broad imaging and stereo capability of side placement, it does minimize the phase cancellations caused by timing differences from separated speakers. It also provides a central **point-source reference** meaning sound is emanating from the location where most of the primary action is.

Combining a central cluster with side placement will create a **left-center-right** (LCR) configuration. This can be difficult in anything other than permanent installs unless sufficient front truss is available overhead. A few major companies make mixing consoles designed for this arrangement, but a 'pseudo' LCR setup can be accomplished with almost any console. One way is to use the stereo out for L-R and a group or matrix output for center. Another way is to forget about running stereo, which isn't important in most live applications, and run Left mixer out to center and Right out to L-R. This way, the channel pan control determines whether a source comes through the center, sides, or a combination of both.

The initial idea with LCR was to maintain more accurate direction of sound consistent with performers' positions on stage, but I believe a more substantial result is better separation between the vocals and the instruments. I use this setup in theatre with sides dedicated to instruments or stereo soundtracks and a slightly more forward center cluster dedicated to the singers/actors, and the quality of sound is superb since they aren't competing with each other through the same speakers. There is also a clarifying imaging difference which simulates natural acoustics: a wide musical group surrounding and behind the front and center singers. I use 15" 2-way speakers with subs for the music and smaller 12" 2-way on vocals for better definition. If you don't have center cluster capability, you could experiment with dedicated vocal speakers split to both sides with the stacks if you have the resources. You just might like it.

[Note: Always make sure elevated speakers are properly suspended and equipped with safety-approved standmount or hanging hardware.]

Monitors: A smooth sound with emphasis in the 500Hz to 5kHz range and good definition at 2-3kHz is important to clarity that can cut through stage levels. Don't try to blast everything; the sound will just get loud and cluttered and nobody will be happy. Compromise with the performers on balancing the more critical parts that need to be heard. If levels start getting out of hand or close to feedback, start backing out the less important stuff to accentuate the priorities and clean up the sound. Roll out low end on the monitor EQs to reduce muddiness. (There will generally be plenty of low end support from the main system.) In-ear or small monitors like Galaxy Hot Spots can also help minimize sound bleed and stage level.

Feedback[4]**:** The best defense is a well-tuned system, hypercardioid mics, and staying within the capabilities of your system and environment. When a consistent feedback area occurs in mains or monitors, locate the one or two sliders on the appropriate graphic EQ that affect it most and *only* lower those slightly. There are typically only two or three spots that need control. Beyond that, you may find yourself progressively dropping *all* your sliders in a snowball effect, losing gain and quality. (More feedback stuff on page 61.) You might consider purchasing a realtime analyzer to help find feedback points, or a feedback suppressor like a Sabine FBX or DBX Pro AFS unit which is designed to automatically find and remove them.

CHURCH SOUND

The church audio environment is almost a contradiction, just like *sound engineer*. (That's *sound* as in "sane, rational, responsible, wise, perceptive, logical, sober!" I rest my case.) That's because church audio can incorporate critical speaking, music production, concerts, theatrical presentations, *and* recording. And who typically runs it all? Volunteers!

On top of that, we have a very discerning and broad audience of 1 to 100 year olds who aren't concerned with technicalities. They just want things to sound good and look nice. I can't think of a more complex situation to be in, unless you're a pastor who *has* a poor sound system. Then prayer is the first step. This section is the second.

Sanctuary Studios: I use this term because church audio is a critical, controlled environment. Once things are set up properly, there's not much need for change, and procedure and operation can be pretty consistent from week to week. Major emphasis should be on logical system design for ease of use, equipment and settings labeled and logged as a constant reference, and one person dedicated to responsibility for operations and related decisions. Too many cooks spoil the broth.

In addition, a well-tuned speaker system will give you an accurate reference as do studio monitors, allowing you to make proper EQ and balance decisions that transfer favorably to any recording or broadcast applications you may have or eventually add.

Speakers: Speaker choices and arrangements are of prime importance. I've seen cheap *and* expensive setups that sounded terrible and only covered half the sanctuary. Obviously, the salesmen or installers didn't have a clue or didn't care. (They may have claimed to be non-denominational, but I'll bet they favored $10's and $20's.)

I suggest 2-way speakers with a horizontal horn *dispersion*[23] of 60° to 75° since these will throw more evenly over distance than a 90°. (*No piezo horns!* Refer to the Speaker section for more guidance.) Horns should be directed towards the rear seating of the sanctuary with the lower, forward edge of the horn pattern catching the first row. If hung in a *central cluster*[24], I favor 12" 2-ways for better vocal definition. Any speaker hung in this 'free field' will lack sub-bass anyway, so add a subwoofer somewhere on the floor or under the staging if strong bass is preferred. If speakers are placed in side chambers, 15" 2-ways without subs can be sufficient due to increased bass efficiency from the walls or boundaries. Side placement can also offer stereo capability and a bigger sound for music and choir, easier access for maintenance, and an often less conspicuous location especially when you have side chambers.

Determining the best position for speakers is a little touchier. Though a central cluster can be a safer bet in most rooms, I find side placement or left-center-right (LCR) configurations as good or better in many average-size facilities. Where I used to believe that a cluster was the only appropriate choice, as many sound consultants still do, I eventually discovered that there were more creative aspects of system design that went beyond theoretical technicalities and into the realm of what I call **acoustical emulation**. In other words, if individual instruments and vocals can *acoustically* exhibit location and timing differences, why can't speakers serve to emulate that? This was the reason for my previous explanation of LCR systems (in the Club & Concert Sound section) as offering clarifying separation and imaging, duplicating similar acoustical characteristics that help our ears distinguish sounds in a 3-dimensional environment.

Another consideration is how *sound energy* is concentrated or distributed. If you have a central cluster hanging only 10' to 15' over a pulpit due to a low ceiling, all the sound energy will be concentrated directly over some of the more feedback prone mics, namely the pastor's lavalier and the podium mic. If instead you place the speakers at a 10' height on each side of the stage, the sound energy is distributed over a wider field reducing the feedback potential at any particular point on stage. If the pastor is standing on the far left, he is only close to half the energy and vice versa. Also, with smaller rooms, you don't have to be overly concerned with point-source reference since the ambient voice itself can provide that. The speakers can merely offer supplemental definition.

Though I encourage you to consult with a professional on speaker system design, I can offer a few of my personal guidelines:

- *Side Mounting* - rooms with lower ceilings and/or up to 60' wide and 80' deep with center aisle (minimizes audible phase cancellation). Speakers should be 10'-15' high, and at least 10' forward of the first row of seats. Will also cover most balconies.
- *Cluster* - rooms with ceilings 20' or higher and/or 60'-100' wide, or those without center aisle or side placement locations. Centered over pulpit, use two speakers arrayed to cover 100° to 120°, three or four for wider seating requiring 180° to 220° coverage. Horns should be at least 15'-20' high depending on depth of room and possible balcony coverage.
- *LCR* - simply a combination of the previous two which I prefer in many larger rooms or those wider than they are deep. Be aware that Center and Left-Right each need to be full coverage. (Can also be used with some lower ceilings since critical mics can be supplemented through the Left-Right speakers to distribute sound energy.)

Rooms seating over 1,000 or those with unusual acoustics (I once evaluated a sanctuary that had so many reflections arriving simultaneously at one spot, it created its own pitch!), or complex balcony or side wing construction will require more strategic design. Some will require a combination of cluster, side fills, and delayed speaker arrangements. Leave it to the professionals unless you're real brave or the church is very forgiving.

Stereo Tracks: You'll notice I mentioned 'stereo-capable' for side placement. I like stereo operation when practical since churches are often using stereo cassette or CD tracks for singers. With cassette, mono systems can cause some high-frequency phase cancellation between the left and right tracks. This is the result of the tape not aligning perfectly on the deck's heads. Stereo operation eliminates any audible problem. If you're not running stereo, use only one side of the cassette output (preferably the left to accommodate the music side of "split tracks"), or run the channel of one side lower than the other to minimize phasing effects.

You can also develop some 'conducting' capabilities for music tracks as if you were leading an orchestra. Make sure the quiet beginnings are raised enough for the singers to get their cues. If dynamics seem to be lacking, you can drop back music slightly during verses and gradually swell the music while the last note is being held. You'd be surprised at the extra impact such subtle changes will add to a performance and an otherwise 'flat' background. If necessary, consult with your music director on these techniques.

Feedback Control[4]: Choir mics and tie-clip lavaliers cause some of the greatest feedback difficulties, and they're good reason to insist on a mixer with at least one sweep frequency in the channel EQ. Without it, you can't address specific problem areas for individual mics. First step is finding and controlling the few major feedback points, thereby smoothing out most of the rough spots. Afterwards, you just have to be mindful that you have some limit to any given mic's level before feedback will start. Assuming you have at least 3-band, sweep mid EQ . . .

Gradually bring up a problem channel until slight, controlled feedback starts. If the feedback tone is a very low or high frequency, cut back the appropriate fixed EQ knob a notch or two. If the tone sounds more in the vocal range, set the mid control at 10:00 and rotate the sweep frequency knob until you hear the feedback dip. Set the sweep at the dip point, then bring up the fader more to find and work out the next feedback point. If it's one of the previous again, drop the appropriate EQ control another notch. If it's a midrange tone close to the first, you may be able to compromise the sweep frequency position along with a little more rolloff to catch them both. Try for a third feedback frequency unless you start getting two or three at once. Then stop. To go further will most likely get you to the point of diminishing returns. Finish up by making subtle EQ adjustments for voice quality if necessary.

With a well-tuned system, I almost always have to roll back somewhere between 400Hz and 800Hz as well as some low end on choir mics and omni lavaliers. The miniature podium condensers may require some similar adjustments. Good handheld mics don't give me any trouble, but piano mics may depending on the level needed from them. Watch your stage monitor levels, too. If there is a consistent problem frequency here, take it down slightly on the monitor graphic EQ. If you have trouble locating feedback consider purchasing a **realtime analyzer** (p. 35). The answers will light up before your very eyes and before long, you'll be able to approximate frequencies by ear.

I have a method for setting level on the most finicky mics to avoid feedback during the service — from the system *and* the pastor. After equalizing, I'll set the channel fader at the nominal "0" (or 2/3 up) position and bring up the input gain until feedback starts, then back off a notch or so. I'll also check choir mics with all their faders up to account for the collective level. This way, I know that "0" is the highest I can safely go on the fader, and any higher will be shaky ground. (And we all know *shaky ground* and *solid rock* don't mix.)

Phase Reverse[14]: There may come a time when a pastor with an active wireless lavalier walks up to an active podium mic, and his voice suddenly becomes very thin or hollow sounding. This is an indication that the two mics are wired out of phase. If you have phase reverse on your mixer, switch it on the podium mic. If not, reverse the hot and neutral on one end of the podium mic cable. This will be easier than attempting a modification to the wireless. Also, due to distance phase effects, it would be best to commit to one mic or the other instead of leaving them both on. Wireless wins if the pastor moves around.

Another phase effect can be caused by sound bouncing into the mics off a hard podium surface. If you notice a problem, try some carpeting on its surface to absorb reflections. (You may be able to get away with light gray or white on a clear plexiglass podium. Clear carpet is very expensive and hard to come by.)

Right-Wing Engineering: The catch word for conservative engineering is sound *reinforcement,* not *replacement.* Think about how close you can stay to natural sound levels rather than how much you can overpower them. In any church, I'll be able to hear at least some of the instruments, singers, and speaker's voice carry acoustically in the room. It just wouldn't be enough to distinguish everything clearly or get over music or background noises. So I add just the level needed to accomplish that. Then sound retains a natural quality and sense of location. As with micing, trust your ear. If you can't hear what's being said, others won't be able to either. If it's loud to you, it's probably blasting grandma in the front row. Use common sense for the common good.

A service can include spontaneous activity from pastors, music leaders, or members of the congregation as they are felt led. Don't be a robot, but be aware of what is going on and prepared to bring up speaking or wireless mics as needed. Most pastors have certain moves they make that indicate they're about to speak, so try to second-guess them. Don't wait until after they start before you bring them up, and don't use channel on/off switches for them. Use the faders for more gradual changes in case you miss a cue.

Concentrate on the main music leader and instrument, normally piano, in the monitors. These will provide the primary vocal, pitch and rhythm reference for all concerned. Be careful about trying to feed choir or lavalier mics through nearby monitors. They're already prone to feedback enough as it is.

Service Recording: Some mixers provide tape outputs for recording, but they are simply paralleled off the main outputs. A convenient way to get an easy and individual recording feed from a stereo mixer (if you're not running stereo) is to use the Left output for live sound and the Right for recording. Separate left and right master faders give you convenient level control for each. If certain channels are too loud on tape, pan them sufficiently to the left reducing their level through the right output. If you use dedicated mics to record the congregation, pan them full right so they only go to tape. Once these compensated recording levels are set, normal operation for the house will balance properly on the recording. This feed is also useful for video recording and hearing-assistance systems as well as peripheral speakers in foyer, halls, nursery, etc. (If you have extra auxes and this left/right method is not available, simply use a post-fader aux send for individual channel control.)

Another relatively new tool in this ministry is CD recording and duplication. I feel churches should be transitioning to this technology since cost has dropped below that of the better cassette duplicators, there are less maintenance costs and concerns, CD quality is much better, blank CDRs are much cheaper than the lowest grade cassette tape, and audio can be transferred easily to computer for archiving, editing, and web access.

Though I'm sure we'll see a lot of creative products in time, one current unit is the Copywriter Live from Microboards which records and duplicates in a self-contained, 2-drive model. In addition to individual recording, the drives offer a continuous-recording mode by automatically overlapping to the next drive before time runs out. You can also record two separate CDs for Service and Sermon by simply pausing and starting individual CDRs at appropriate points in the program. (This is great if you wish to record a complete service that exceeds 80 minutes, the max time for a 700MB CD.) Add an 8-drive tower duplicator, and you can run off high quantities of CDs in house. *(Note: Be aware of laws about duplicating copyrighted music from church programs. Contact artists or licensing organizations about restrictions and approvals.)*

Following are some final notes:

- Choose a mixer with phantom power and at least one sweep EQ on channels.
- Always buy low impedance mics. (These use XLR, not 1/4" phone plugs.)
- Use a quick-reverse cassette deck for recording so you don't miss anything.
- For safety, consider mounting a *wireless* mic in the baptismal when needed.
- Don't buy PA speakers with 'piezo' horns. For stage monitors, they'll do.
- Always make sure elevated speakers are properly suspended and equipped with safety-approved standmount or hanging hardware.
- Always commend the worship leader on how lovely (he/she) looks today.

THEATRICAL SOUND

Theatre is very similar to church in that natural sound quality is a priority, especially with all the speaking parts involved. Careful consideration should be given to the natural blend of ambient and reinforced sound. A speaker combination of central cluster (for vocals) and stereo side arrangements (for score) can be ideal for musicals in larger venues, especially with pre-recorded or sequenced tracks, and may not be too difficult given the flexibility of many stage layouts. This serves to separate the music and voices for better sound and imaging.

I also address this application specifically because of the potential number of wireless employed and the problems of amplifying all the critical dialog or singing with numerous mics. Unfortunately, the distance and movement of actors onstage renders fixed mic pickup extremely difficult. A stagefront floor-mounted unidirectional boundary mic like the Crown PCC-160 or a hanging choir mic can be reasonably effective for picking up individuals within an 8' square or group speaking or singing within 15' if the system is tuned well and the actors can project and e-n-u-n-c-i-a-t-e. Otherwise, wireless lavalier mics are going to be your best bet.

For most situations including churches and schools, $300 to $600 VHF wireless by such companies as Audio-Technica, Azden, and Shure do very well. You'll always need to be careful of damage to transmitter parts and cable connections, and you should keep receivers elevated and within 75' of the stage if possible to avoid dropouts. Arrange workable mic passes to other actors if you're short a few systems. You could also purchase extra mics which can be precisely placed on performers ahead of time, and just exchange transmitters for quicker mic passes.

For more critical applications, the over $1000 UHF systems are a definite plus due to their tighter reception which allows a greater number of systems to be used without interference problems. UHF has become more affordable and most are equipped with a number of selectable frequencies, but models under $1000 are typically limited to twelve or less compatible channels like VHF. When you need more and cost savings too, you can mix economical UHF and VHF together.

Lavalier mics are often worn on the chest, but can also be hidden in the hair or placed over the ear. In the absence of sinus problems, nostril placement offers excellent pickup if you can successfully hide the cable. (Now truthfully, how many of you actually considered this for a second?) I have also been able to spraypaint mics and cables with Krylon to match hair, flesh, or clothing colors, but be sure to cover the mic element and plugs while doing so. The paint can usually be removed with alcohol if you need a color change later, but be aware that alcohol can damage rubber parts if used too much. Best to test paint and removal on an inconspicuous section of cable before proceeding.

With the physical nature of some dramatic productions, be ready for potential problems caused by perspiration getting into mic connections. To remedy this, place the mic in a dry area or seal vulnerable connections with silicone sealer. Another important preventative is to tape over transmitter and mic on/off switches so they don't accidentally get switched off during a performance. Leave the on/off indicator visible if possible, and use gaffer's tape (not masking or duct tape) to avoid sticky glue buildup on the transmitter. You may also want to tape down non-locking mic plugs.

When engineering for the theatre, you've got to stay on top of the dialog and make script notations accordingly. I notate mic numbers in the script margins in place of names when mic passes are involved. Circling the number where the actor first enters is a good mic cue, and a "# Off" where they exit makes sure they aren't live offstage. In a particular scene, I'll have all the appropriate mics up to moderate levels and ride them up and down as lines are spoken. Be sure to notate loud passages like yells, screams, whistles, etc. for a quick adjustment to avoid a few migraines in the audience.

You'll also notice that actors can be picked up through each other's mics if they are close to one another. To minimize the resulting effects, either ride their mics up and down accordingly or commit to one mic if there is little movement between the actors. As you become familiar with the parts and dialogue, you can actually get into a rhythm just as the actors do. If there are prerecorded music and sound effects, try to have someone else control them to keep you free for the wireless. It takes good script notes and some practice, but it's a rewarding feeling when the spontaneous spirit of engineering and dramatic performance come together as one soul-stirring entity.

SO, DO I HAVE TO PAINT YOU A PICTURE?

I guess you thought I'd forget! Yes, I understand how difficult it can be to put the whole thing together without a chart. I, too, have tried putting together Christmas toys! (Take my word for it, audio is easier.) So as a final touch, I've included a graphic diagram of a complete sound system on the next page with the major components, their page locations, and indications of connections and signal flow. Illustrations such as this are provided in many mixer manuals (and should be), so refer to them for more specific information and other applications.

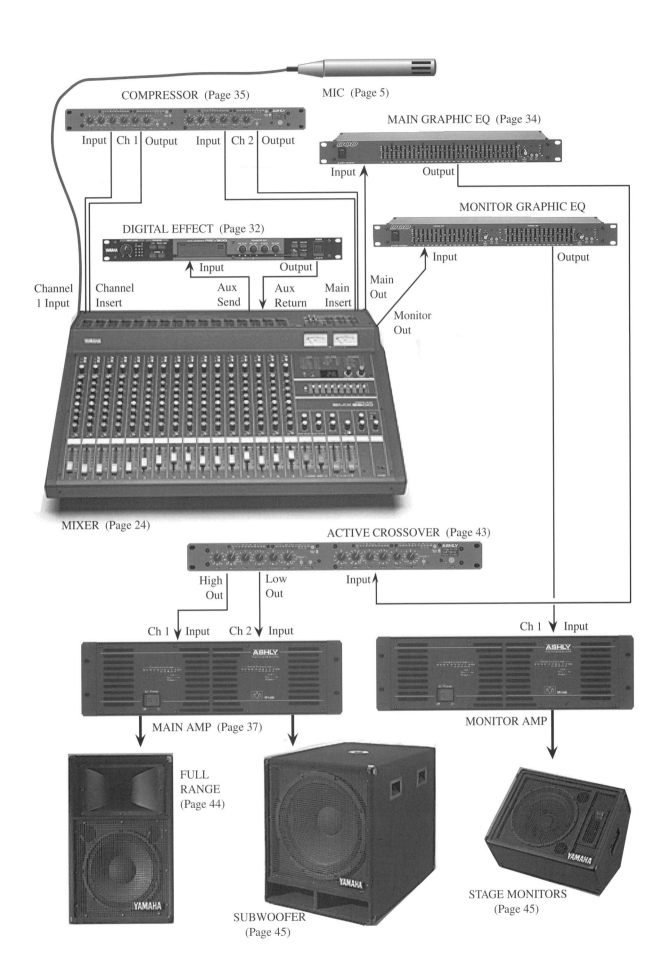

COMPRESSOR (Page 35) MIC (Page 5)

MAIN GRAPHIC EQ (Page 34)

Input Ch 1 Output Input Ch 2 Output

Input Output

DIGITAL EFFECT (Page 32)

MONITOR GRAPHIC EQ

Input Output

Channel
1 Input

Channel
Insert

Aux
Send

Aux
Return

Main
Insert

Main
Out

Monitor
Out

MIXER (Page 24)

ACTIVE CROSSOVER (Page 43)

High
Out

Low
Out

Input

Ch 1 Input Ch 2 Input

Ch 1 Input

MAIN AMP (Page 37)

MONITOR AMP

FULL
RANGE
(Page 44)

STAGE MONITORS
(Page 45)

SUBWOOFER
(Page 45)

13. PACKING UP

Well, I think I've covered about everything I wanted to and, quite frankly, I've run out of words. I pretty much stayed with what was in my head (as opposed to other areas), and I can't begin to remember where it all came from. A lot of trial and error, and a few major screw-ups for sure. And it surprised me almost as much as my wife that this much stuff was actually in my head!

There are lots of good books that specialize in various areas of audio, and I encourage you to pursue them as your desire dictates. I hope I've provided you with an abundance of valuable information here. If not, I probably won't retire at age fifty with lots of money, so I'll settle for fifty-five and a stash of McDonald's coupons. Good luck to you, too. I trust you'll enjoy the same satisfaction and rewards that I have in this exciting, challenging, and ever-changing world of pro audio. Take your time, and thank you for giving me some of it.

"There's no business like show business, like no business I know . . ."

P.S. I wouldn't want to disappoint those of you who thought this section was about packing up equipment: "Don't scratch anything and put the heavy stuff up front."

For those of you who may wish to contact me with questions, comments, or critique (be gentle), address correspondence to:

Ira White c/o Sanctuary Sound
5660 E. Virginia Beach Blvd.
Norfolk, VA 23502
Email: iwhite@specialtyproducts.net

INDEX (in order of appearance)

ABOUT THE AUTHOR

    Ira white has been involved in the music business since 1971. Born in Norfolk, Virginia, he began playing professionally as a guitarist/singer in various touring bands. He put together his first 8-track personal studio in 1983, which eventually expanded into a 16-track commercial production facility. Work in retail music sales as well as live recording and sound engineering in concert. theatre, and church venues were a progressive outgrowth of his interests and contacts.

    In 1992, he started Studio Street in Virginia Beach, a pro audio store and consulting/install firm which evolved into Sanctuary Sound, Inc. He also works as sound director for a local church, serves occasionally as worship leader, and is still involved as an independent producer/engineer, songwriter, and studio guitarist. Recent projects have included *TMCJ International* theatrical productions and the *Lion of Judah* tour for worship artist Paul Wilbur.

    Ira resides in Portsmouth, VA with his wife Susan. His hobbies are scuba diving, camping, and discussing audio with his dogs who have excellent high frequency perception.